WALK WITH ME

A JOURNEY TO FULL FREEDOM FROM AN EATING DISORDER

VANESSA SCHÖN

DENVER, COLORADO

Outskirts Press, Inc.
http://www.outskirtspress.com

ISBN: 978-1-4787-2353-0

Outskirts Press and the "OP" logo are trademarks belonging to Outskirts Press, Inc.

PRINTED IN THE UNITED STATES OF AMERICA

For my mother, Silvia Martín del Campo

For walking with me every step of the way.

For Jorge "Coke" Villarreal

For being a light in my life.

For Tita

For always wanting the best and nothing less for me.

I carry you in my heart, always.

Table of Contents

Foreword

Approximately 20 million women and 10 million men suffer from a clinically significant eating disorder (ED)* *in the United States alone* (Wade, K., & Hudson, 2011). Along with many misconceptions about eating disorders, they have little to do with dieting. Although eating disorders may begin with preoccupations about food and weight, *they are about so much more than that.* Eating disorders are life-threatening medical and psychiatric disorders which require extensive treatment.

Contrary to other popular beliefs, eating disorders are not a choice, a quest for vanity, or a "phase" people go through. As stated by the National Association of Anorexia Nervosa and Associated Disorders (ANAD), a person cannot simply "catch" an eating disorder for a period of time, just like someone does not choose to get cancer or go through a "phase" of diabetes.

Eating disorders are real, complex, and life-threatening illnesses. They have the highest mortality rate of *any* mental illness. Today, anorexia nervosa is the third most common chronic illness among adolescents ("Eating Disorder Statistics," 2013). The mortality rate associated with it is 12 times higher than the death rate associated with all causes of death for females 15–24 years old (2013). Children as young as 5 can begin struggling with bulimia nervosa, the second-most common eating disorder among young adults. There are several different types and subtypes of eating disorders, all of which are serious and require professional treatment, like any illness does.

Eating disorders do not "target" people of certain social classes, race, or ethnicity. Eating disorders *do not discriminate*. They affect people of all ages, gender, and backgrounds. Another misconception about eating disorders is that they only affect women. This is far from true. According to the South Carolina Department of Mental Health, an estimated 10–15 percent of people with anorexia or bulimia are males, and this number has continued to increase with time (2006). The belief that eating disorders are a "woman's disease" often keep males from seeking treatment (2006).

One of the most common misconceptions that exists about eating disorders is that in order for a person to be sick they have to be emaciated to a point where they are near death. *Weight* is not necessarily an indicator of whether one struggles with an eating disorder. In fact, according to experts, "because many individuals with bulimia maintain normal or above-normal body weight, they can often successfully hide their problem from others for years" ("Bulimia Symptoms, 2013). An eating disorder is a **mental illness** "that manifests itself in eating symptoms and subsequent weight changes," with many factors contributing to their development (Gallagher, 2012). These include biological, social, psychological, and interpersonal factors. This is what makes their treatment and understanding so complex.

At the same time, with more information as to what contributes to their development, heightened awareness, and advances in psychology, neuroscience, and medicine, earlier prevention and more efficient treatment options are becoming available for patients and their loved ones.

Factors

Eating disorders are complex conditions that arise from a combination of long-standing behavioral, biological, emotional, psychological, interpersonal, and social factors. Scientists and researchers are still learning about the underlying causes of these emotionally and physically damaging conditions. We do know, however, about some of the general issues that can contribute to the development of eating disorders.

While eating disorders may begin with preoccupations with food and weight, they are most often about much more than food. People with eating disorders often use food and the control of food in an attempt to compensate for feelings and emotions that may otherwise seem overwhelming. For some, dieting, bingeing, and purging may begin as a way to cope with painful emotions and to feel in control of one's life, but ultimately, these behaviors will damage a person's physical and emotional health, self-esteem, and sense of competence and control.

Psychological Factors that Can Contribute to Eating Disorders:
- Low self-esteem
- Feelings of inadequacy or lack of control in life
- Depression, anxiety, anger, or loneliness

Interpersonal Factors that Can Contribute to Eating Disorders:

- Troubled personal relationships
- Difficulty expressing emotions and feelings
- History of being teased or ridiculed based on size or weight
- History of physical or sexual abuse

Social Factors that Can Contribute to Eating Disorders:

- Cultural pressures that glorify "thinness" and place value on obtaining the "perfect body"
- Narrow definitions of beauty that include only women and men of specific body weights and shapes
- Cultural norms that value people on the basis of physical appearance and not inner qualities and strengths

Biological Factors that Can Contribute to Eating Disorders:

- Scientists are still researching possible biochemical or biological causes of eating disorders. In some individuals with eating disorders, certain chemicals in the brain that control hunger, appetite, and digestion have been found to be unbalanced. The exact meaning and implications of these imbalances remain under investigation.
- Eating disorders often run in families. Current research indicates that there are significant genetic contributions to eating disorders.

*Eating disorders are complex conditions that can arise from a variety of potential causes. Once started, however, they can create a self-perpetuating cycle of physical and emotional destruction. **All eating disorders require professional help.**

Source: National Eating Disorders Association[1]

---

1 Factors that May Contribute to Eating Disorders. (n.d.). Retrieved January 5, 2012, from http://www.nationaleatingdisorders.org/uploads/file/informationresoyources/Factors%20that%20%may%20%Contribute%20to%20%Eating%Disorders.pdf

A Growing Problem

The prevalence of eating disorders continues to increase at an alarming, epidemic rate. Statistics gathered by the National Association of Anorexia Nervosa and Associated Disorders (ANAD) in 2012 give us the following facts:

- The body type portrayed in advertising as the ideal is possessed naturally by only 5 percent of American females.
- 35 percent of "normal dieters" progress to pathological dieting. Of those, 20–25 percent progress to partial or full-syndrome eating disorders.
- 47 percent of girls in 5th–12th grade reported wanting to lose weight because of magazine pictures.
- 69 percent of girls in 5th–12th grade reported that magazine pictures influenced their idea of a perfect body shape.
- 42 percent of 1st–3rd-grade girls want to be thinner.
- 81 percent of 10-year-olds are afraid of being fat.

According to the National Eating Disorders Association, "40–60 percent of elementary schoolgirls (ages 6–12) are concerned about their weight or about becoming too fat" ("Going to Extremes: Eating

Disorders, 2012"). "From 1999 to 2006, eating-disorder related hospitalizations increased 18 percent overall, 37 percent among men and 119 percent among children under 12 years old" (2012).

What has caused this dramatic spike in the occurrence of eating disorders? Experts believe that society and cultural pressures are to blame. Jan Lockert, RN, eating disorder survivor and Director of Admissions and Outreach at the River Centre Clinic for Eating Disorders in Toledo, Ohio, offers her input:

"As it's impossible to identify only one causative factor in the development of an eating disorder, I believe it's impossible that one factor has led to an increase in the number of people suffering from eating disorders. Our Western society, with the strong focus on appearance and acceptance of dieting as a lifestyle, are definitely important factors. I also believe that we are now seeing more 'generational' affects, not only in terms of genetics, but also environmental, where daughters of mothers who suffered in their younger years, or may still be suffering, are now seeking help. Another factor that we are seeing emerge, is the 'glamorizing' of eating disorders that some identify with."

Knowing that several factors take must place in order for an eating disorder to occur, what can be done to turn these statistics around? According to Lockert, "I think the emotional factors can be addressed early in life, which could possibly decrease the amount of eating disorders that eventually develop, such as self-worth and esteem, anxiety, body acceptance, emotional flexibility, unconditional acceptance, emotional expression, and so forth."

We can all do our part to help those struggling and prevent many from falling ill to these devastating illnesses. No one deserves to suffer with an eating disorder. These illnesses are *treatable and preventable*. Lockert adds, "Early intervention certainly shortens the duration of illness and decreases risk for long-term medical consequences."

If you or someone you know is suffering from an eating disorder, know that there are hope and treatment options available. For information on treatment options, resources, and hotlines, visit the "Resources" section at the end of this book. You are not alone. There is hope, support, and help available. You can recover from an eating disorder, and you can recover completely. I say this with conviction.

Join me in the fight against eating disorders.
Walk with me.

Acknowledgments

I could not have written this book if it weren't for some amazing individuals. More important, I could not have gotten to where I am today had it not been for each and every one of them. I have a lot of people to thank.

I would like to thank the two professionals who stood by me when I first began my journey of recovery. My former therapist, Natalie H. Frost, MS, LPC; and psychiatrist, Pamela A. Dunkin, MD.

I would like to thank Victoria Lee Spring for being a huge inspiration for me in recovery. She showed me through example that full recovery from an eating disorder was possible, exemplifying courage, persistence, and the will to never give up. I always remember a quote by Robert Frost that Victoria would repeat often: "It's never too late to be who you might have been." Thank you, Victoria.

I absolutely cannot express enough gratitude and appreciation toward the treatment team who worked with me throughout the most vital part of my recovery, the individuals at Tapestry Treatment Center in Brevard, North Carolina. They provided me the tools to build a strong foundation which I needed in order to recover fully. Thank you for everything: Tina Nowak, R.N., Sadie Carlson, MA, MFT; Leslie Laney, R.D.; Nicole Fahy, MA, LPC, NCC; Heidi Houser, MS, LPC;

Ward Johnson, MA MFCC–EMDR/DBT; Kathy Jones; Kathleen A. Menk Krupar; Martha "Martita" Rogers; and Kristen Johnson. Thank you to each of the residential counselors for the laughter, the support, and the joy you brought into my life when I so desperately needed it: Tammy Maxey, Pam Sanders, Samantha McGuire, Karen George, Margaret Ann "Oslo" Medley, Ladonna Huffaker, Caitlin Coffey, and Bridget Johnson.

I would like to express my greatest appreciation to the group of professionals who helped me break through the final battles against my eating disorder and later became mentors to me as I transitioned into the workfield. Thank you: Lorena Calderón Flores, Dr. Isabel Kuthy and Ari Ortega.

A quote I love by Oprah Winfrey says, "Surround yourself by people who are only going to lift you higher." I am grateful and so fortunate for my friends who stood by me (and many times helped me stand up) during my most difficult days. I love you guys: Kevin Kuyosu, Kathyrn Powell, Adam Matthews, Timm and Elizabeth Tilson, Grace Welsh, Kamren Kowa, and Martha Sainz. Special thanks to Gaby de la Piedra and Mauricio Melendes for believing in me, and the children who showed me hope, happiness, and genuine love at Victoria's Kindergarten School in Cancun, Q. Roo.

From the bottom of my heart, I would like to thank all of my family—my aunts, uncles, and cousins. An enormous wave of love, gratitude, and thanks to all of you for all of your kindnesses, words of advice, love, and support. Special thanks to Adrian Carabias and his family for believing in me and cheering me on throughout the publication process of this book. I would also like to thank my friends, my professors, and fellow students at the University of Anáhuac in Cancún, Quintana Roo.

Without a doubt, my greatest pillar of strength in my life has been my mother, Silvia. There aren't enough words I could ever write to express how grateful, fortunate, and blessed I am to have her as my mother. Since day one of my recovery, she told me that she would always *walk with me* on this journey. She promised to always walk by my side, holding my hand through the entire process. Ten years since making that promise to me, she has continued to keep her word. I want to thank her for her unconditional support *through it all*, for her immense love, for being an incredible mother, and my best friend. The grace, courage, and attitude she carries with her so elegantly are something I admire greatly. Thank you for everything, Mom. I love you.

I would like to thank my stepdad, Oscar, for all of his support, kindnesses, and words of wisdom. He helped me make the most important decision in my life when he suggested residential treatment for my eating disorder. Only God knows how much longer I could have gone or where I would be today had I not sought out help at that point. Oscar is a wonderful and honest human being, with an enormous heart. I am thankful for his continuous support and admire him greatly.

I want to thank the two people I care about the most. These are the two people who give the most meaning to my life—to my existence even before birth. My right and left arm, Stephy and Nicky. Words cannot express how much they mean to me, how much I look up to them, and how much they have helped me in my recovery and continue to support me in my journey of life. Thank you for *always* being by my side. For supporting me and encouraging me. Thank you for sticking by me through the good and the bad—the pain, the struggles, and the frustration—time and time again. Nicky, for your patience and insight; and Stephy, for slapping me with reality in the face when I needed it. Both of you stood by me as I fought through an eating disorder, and together, I know we will continue to conquer any obstacles that life throws at us.

I'd like to thank my dad, Benito, whose lessons he taught me began as a kid, and so many of them on the tennis court. The skills I learned on the court served purpose for me much further than that—throughout my entire recovery and life to this day. I learned early on that the game of life, on and off the court, is *99 percent mental*. He showed me dedication and ingrained consistency day in and day out into my life, tools which were essential for me to overcome my illness. He taught me to *never give up* and always told me I was a fighter. I held on to those words always, even when I felt no hope inside of me, or couldn't see any way out of the situation I was in.

I continued to fight. I continued to choose recovery. And I made it. *Thank you.*

I would like to give the warmest, most sincere message of appreciation to all of my nonbiological sisters, my sisters in recovery. From the bottom of my heart, *thank you.* I could not have made it through recovery had it not been for every one of you. We managed to find light and humor in our situation despite difficult moments. (Like Ward once said to a group of us in therapy, "these are the best of times; these are the worst of times.") I couldn't have asked for greater companions. Together, we walked the road of recovery, fought, fell, and picked each other up. I am grateful for each and every one of you. You are all incredible, intelligent, wonderful human beings. You all mean so much to me. *Stay strong and keep fighting every day for the freedom and life you deserve:*

Sarah C.
Madelyn L.
Lauren M.
Susannah F.
Caitlin W.
Kimberly J.
Ashli S.
Carey M.
Heather P.
Tonya C.
Joanna A.
Kristina Z.
Jennifer L.
Kathy M.
Angela
Nina C.
Molly P.
Jenna H.
Paula T.
Autumn B.
Kimberly M.

Lauren M.
Kimberly G.
Kimberly
Jen J.
Lize V.
Bailey W.
Stacie M.
Lauren Ashley T.
Lindsey P.
Jessica M.
Ashley P.
Tina Z.
Sheila W.
Joan
Fer P.
Brittany B.
Fernanda C.
Stephanie F.

Lastly, I would like to thank every brave warrior fighting the war against eating disorders. Thank you to every survivor, professional, family member, friend, and organization doing their part to help those struggling. Thanks to so many of you, I was provided with resources, words of insight, and support that made the difference in pushing through moments when I felt utterly alone. There are many people out there who have provided me with wise words, insight, and support who I do not have the privilege to know in person. I didn't always have an "ideal" support system surrounding me. Thanks to their support, I was able to break through many barriers in recovery. *Thank you.*

What This Book Is All About

There have been many books written on eating disorders. Books that list symptoms, diagnoses, development, and consequences of eating disorders. Books that highlight the growing prevalence, statistics, and offer the latest investigations in neuroscience, psychology, and medicine that are offering new treatment options and more insight into the area. This is excellent, valuable information. These books help raise awareness, counteract stigmas and misconceptions commonly associated with eating disorders, and provide readers with up-to-date information on current investigations.

There are also a handful of testimonies written by survivors. These books often go into great depth describing the agony the victim encountered during the grips of their illness, and in some cases, their recovery. These books provide a great deal of insight into the eating disorder sufferer's mind, an unknown territory to those who have not lived the torment of an eating disorder. I applaud every one of the individuals who has the courage and willingness to share something so personal and difficult to describe.

When I was struggling, however, I found myself reading books and articles and always reaching the same conclusion: *now what?* I became overwhelmed with so much information. I was well aware that I had an eating disorder; I knew all of my symptoms matched the classification for anorexia nervosa and major depression. I could list statistics off the top of my head. I knew all of the health risks and consequences associated with the illness. My eating disorder was causing me physical, mental, and emotional pain, and I realized that. I knew that I needed help to get better. But I didn't know *where to go to from there*. I didn't understand how to move forward in the day-to-day process—how or where to even begin.

> *How do I begin recovery? Where do I start? How do I recover? What do I do? What can help me most to recover? Do I really have an eating disorder, or can I actually control this? What do I need to do to recover? Can I recover completely? Does full recovery even exist? What about relapses? What happens if I relapse? How long will this take? Does life without an eating disorder exist for me? Do I even want to recover? Can I?*

These were only some of the questions that came into my head when I first sought out help. My purpose of this book is to give you the answers to those questions. The forward of this book reveals truths—often hard-to-hear realities about eating disorders. Let there be no doubt that **eating disorders are real, complex, and life-threatening illnesses**. However, I will reemphasize that eating disorders are 100 percent *treatable and preventable*. With that, this book is written on a much more optimistic note, without taking away the realness from what we are dealing with.

This book, then, highlights the following points:
- The most useful tools in my recovery after struggling with an eating disorder for 7 years

Eating disorders are already complex, irrational, and manic illnesses. Recovery itself can feel like a roller coaster that just doesn't end. My goal is to make this book as clear and concise as possible. I do my best to be straightforward, direct, and completely honest.

- I will share with you the tools which have saved me from this illness, propelled me and moved me forward in recovery, and got me to where I am today—fully recovered. And maintain a solid state of full recovery.

With an eating disorder you are living to die, you are not living to live.

When I was sick I was living to die. I wore a mask all day in attempt to hide myself from the world; in the end, I couldn't bear wearing it anymore. I took it off and looked myself in the eyes, scared, lost, and more vulnerable than ever—but real. I fearfully walked into my first therapy session in December of 2008 and began my journey back to myself. My goal from then on was to find purpose, joy, and health in my life; to recover myself. Today, 5 years later, I have reached that point. I am now *living to live*. I will share with you in this book how I got to this point.

I am grateful for recovery. I could've easily added "Recovery" to the top of my Acknowledgments section. Thanks to recovery, I was able to recover the most important thing I could ever ask for—myself. And as I got healthier and healthier, everything else that I had been missing out on in life started to fall back into place around me—family, friends, hobbies, passions, the will to live. Recovery was an opportunity that offered me everything in return. I had nothing to lose. With my eating disorder, I had everything to lose. It was my choices, day in and day out, and hard work that would make the difference. I learned that you get out of recovery what you put into it.

Eating disorders promise to give you everything you want, but instead, they take away everything you need.

I am no longer ashamed of sharing my story and speaking my truth. I am thankful for everything recovery has given me. I am incredibly proud of how far I have come, and I am more than happy to share with others how I got to this point. If this book can help at least one person in their recovery, then I can happily say that I accomplished more than I could ask for.

You *can* recover from an eating disorder, and you can recover *completely*. Is recovery difficult? Yes. Impossible? No. I thought I would never recover. I thought this for a long time, even while I was already in recovery and many times making healthy decisions even while not knowing if I would really ever get better. Even when I didn't believe I would get better, I made a promise to myself that I would keep fighting and keep choosing recovery no matter what. I made a promise to myself that I would *never give up*. Kate Le Page, eating disorder survivor and author of *GoodBye Ana*, said in her book that "my worst days in recovery are better than my best days in relapse." Since day 1 of my recovery, I always found that to be true.

I realized I had nothing to lose by giving recovery a shot. When I was sick, I was miserable, lost, detached from life. I was extremely depressed. I lost contact with my friends and was isolated from my family. I avoided so much to the point where going out was not an option since some way or another it would involve food (food is such a wonderful and everyday part of life). Like a quote I came across says, "No one that hates food loves life." I was bombarded with thoughts of food, weight, calories, and starvation all day. I was blinded by my own illness and could not see or think anywhere further than beyond it. It was a living hell. I was living in hell, and I was dying. Many kidnapping victims experience Stockholm syndrome, or capture bonding, a "psychological phenomenon in which hostages express empathy and sympathy and have positive feelings toward their captors, sometimes to the point of defending them. These feelings are generally considered irrational in light of the danger or risk endured by the victims, who essentially mistake a lack of abuse from their captors for an act of kindness ("Possible examples of Stockholm Syndrome," 2012)." Similarly, I was "in love" with my illness, blinded by it, hypnotized by it, and attached to it. For years, I felt like I could never live without my eating disorder, as miserable as I was. I spent years chasing its unfulfilling promises and lies, believing that somehow I would be happy, successful, or "good enough" if I would listen to it. Time passed, years passed, and I began to have glimpses through my own eyes and realize that not only was I was chasing a vapor trail—I was falling into a dark, dark hole. I was losing myself. My illness became my identity, and I didn't know who I was anymore. In those glimpses of reality, I feared I had gone too far—I believed I would never experience life again outside of an eating disorder.

My eating disorder only led me to inner darkness, isolation from the world, lonely hospital visits, and a residential eating disorder clinic. I hit rock bottom time and time again. In the end, my eating disorder would always give me the same results—hospital scares, physical, mental, and emotional torment, and utter loneliness. The risk of losing my life to the illness was always a possibility as well.

I remember one night in my mind very clearly. I was 18 and had just sought out treatment for the first time. I was very sick. I started experiencing severe chest pains one night. My whole family was with me, my sisters were studying at the same university as I was, and my parents had flown from Mexico after hearing about how ill I was.

I remember that night, my parents, sisters, and one of my sister's boyfriends all packed inside a van with me, everyone anxiously muttering trying to find the nearest hospital. We found it, and I walked straight into the ER with my parents.

Shortly after, a nurse called me into one of the back rooms. My mom followed me. Only one person was allowed to accompany me. I remember walking past my sister and my dad at that point, who were sitting on a couch crying. My soul broke into pieces. *This illness is killing my family*, I thought.

I walked to a room in the ER with my mom, and then changed into a hospital gown and sat on the bed. I remember those moments so clearly. It was just my mom and I for those first few minutes. I looked at her, and she looked straight into my eyes, her eyes sad and broken for me. I looked around me. Looked around the room, at the hospital equipment, the white bed, down at my own, thin, sick arms, the gown I was wearing. I remember turning to my mom and telling her,

"This is it."

"This is what?" she said back to me.

"This is everything ED promised me." My mom and I in the emergency room on a Saturday night. All of my friends were out having a great time and enjoying college, their youth. And there I was, sitting on a cold, empty hospital bed with my mom beside me, utterly devastated; my sisters and Dad outside—crying and praying that I didn't have heart damage.

I long dreamed to become a doctor. I remember also thinking that I had always wanted to be in a hospital—but never the patient. This isn't how I wanted my life to be.

What's going to happen next? I asked myself. *What's going to happen if I continue in my eating disorder?*

As ill as I was at that point, I continued to have healthy thoughts (which I identified as my own self speaking) despite the countless unhealthy (eating disorder) thoughts. I knew I needed help, and I wanted to get better. I definitely didn't want to continue in my eating disorder. At the same time, when I was bombarded with eating disorder thoughts it was easy for me to be susceptible to *listening* to those thoughts and believing them to be true (i.e., "If you continue to lose weight you will be in control," "If you don't eat you will feel better," etc.). They are completely irrational thoughts, but only being in recovery for a while was I able to understand the complete nature of the illness.

I was fortunate to walk out of the hospital that day. I told my parents I needed help and thought the best thing for me was to go to residential treatment. As my mind battled between my own voice that wanted help and the eating disorder voice that tried to convince me to stay ill, I told them as soon as I got home that night to remember my words, that *I* agreed to go to treatment—because the next day I might say something different if I was persuaded by the thoughts of my illness.

The next day, I had an appointment set up at a treatment center about an hour away from where I was. I walked in those doors, not knowing what would come next, or who I would be when I walked out of there, but I knew I was more than 100 percent ready to leave behind what had taken my life to that point. I was ready to get help and willing to do whatever I had to do to be well again, to recover myself.

As long as you keep walking the recovery path and pick yourself up after every setback—**you can recover**. A quote by Jim Rohn illustrates this perfectly: *"How long should you try? Until."* Every step you take forward in your recovery will bring you strength you didn't know you had. You will gain insight into yourself, confidence, and get better at recovery as you work on healing yourself and acquire tools along the way. Maybe it's not so much about recovery becoming "easier" as much as it is about you getting stronger.

If you have a slip, it won't be so difficult to get back on your feet as you continue your journey. With each slip, you will be able to get up, quicker each time, and continue forward on your journey with more understanding and knowledge than before. Stumbling blocks will become stepping-stones. Slips will become opportunities for learning and growth. Depression, an opportunity of reflection and insight. And relapse will mean that you still have some things to work on. You will come back stronger with each adversity that you may encounter. Remember, "a smooth sea never made a skillful sailor." And the best thing is, you can choose to get back on the recovery track at any given moment.

Keep putting one foot in front of the other, and no matter what, *never give up* on yourself. If you fall, it's okay (this is a process), just as long as you get back on your feet every time and keep moving forward. *One step at a time*. If you never give up, I guarantee you that you can break free from your eating disorder.

Take a step forward.
Join me on this journey to freedom.
Walk with me.

*"Because if you've found meaning in your life,
you don't want to go back. You want to go forward."*
—Mitch Albom, "Tuesdays with Morrie"

1

Honesty 100 Percent

"Our lives improve only when we take chances—and the first and most difficult risk we can take is to be honest with ourselves."
—Walter Anderson

The only way I was able to ask for help and get treatment was to be completely honest with myself, first and foremost. I remember crying on my bathroom floor in my college dorm. I was at a very low point in my eating disorder. Seven years into it, I was exhausted, desperate, and completely hopeless. I didn't see any way out.

I was 100 percent honest with myself. I fully accepted that I needed help. I accepted that I had a problem, an addiction or an illness, which was out of my control. I knew nothing about recovery, how to or where to find help, or what treatment even entailed. I knew that I couldn't do this anymore, and I needed help to get better. In August of 2008, with the support of my family, I began searching for options. I was in college and far from home, but they encouraged me to look for what I needed. I immediately made an appointment at my school counseling center the next day. They redirected me to an eating disorder therapist close by, an eating disorder support group, and psychiatrist. That is where I began my search for wellness.

Eating disorders *thrive in secrecy.* In order to recover from your eating disorder, you need to be 100 percent honest with yourself and with your treatment team. The best advice I received in early recovery was to **be 100 percent honest**. The first time I walked into residential treatment in October of 2009, I had those words written on my hand. I made it a habit to write those words on my hand throughout my stay there. Later, I made it a habit to write them in my heart.

Being honest is not always easy. Especially in early recovery, or when you are having a difficult time fighting your eating disorder; it *sucks* (for lack of a better word). There is a quote that says, "The truth will set you free, but at first it will make you miserable." I find this to be so true in eating disorder recovery. Being honest in recovery can feel incredibly *uncomfortable* and *foreign* at first. If you feel miserable, vulnerable, angry, uncomfortable, ashamed, and so forth, remember, it is really your eating disorder that is angry, vulnerable, uncomfortable, and upset. You are stripping your illness of its power by taking away its strength, its weapon where it can thrive—*secrecy*.

I like another quote that says, "*We are only as sick as our secrets.*" By being 100 percent honest, you will get the most out of treatment and recovery. Notice I say 100 percent honest. Not 97 percent or 99 percent honest. You have to be *completely* honest about what you are feeling, thinking, and doing in recovery (engaging in behaviors, etc.) with yourself and with your treatment team in order to get well. Don't feel pressured to go up to everyone you know and let them know you are struggling. As long as your treatment team is aware of how you are doing, as long as you keep being honest with them, that is sufficient. Choose one person—your therapist, nutritionist—and stay accountable to them.

In recovery, every little detail adds up. Things that may seem like no big deal can turn into a big deal (like relapse)—had they not been properly in the moment. For example, skipping a snack on your meal plan "here and there" may seem like a minor detail that you don't need to mention to your treatment team. If you are not honest with your team when something like this happens, you are "feeding" your eating disorder. You are giving it power. The more you listen to it (feed it), the stronger it grows. Little slips "here and there" can lead dangerously back to relapse.

By being completely honest, even if you can't catch your eating disorder creeping in, your treatment team and support network can. If you are dishonest, you are only hurting yourself—you have less people to help fight your eating disorder. Don't put yourself at a disadvantage. Make it a point to always be completely honest about your recovery. With time, you can develop a strong sense of awareness and immediately take action when you start to notice yourself slip. In the meantime, however, it can be just as effective to have someone else call your eating disorder out. Your therapist, nutritionist, or psychiatrist can help you overcome your eating disorder, but they are not mind readers. Do not risk depriving yourself of the help you deserve by not being completely honest.

By **practicing honesty at all times during my recovery,** I was able to build upon a solid foundation. When I was at my lowest points, both in my eating disorder and depression, reaching out and being honest with my team **greatly accelerated** my stabilization. By no means am I perfect. I wasn't always honest when I was struggling—and the only thing I "accomplished" by doing so was struggling for a longer period of time, usually getting worse and worse, until I reached a point where being honest was the only thing that could pull me out of the depths I had fallen into. By being honest with my team, they were able to provide much more aimed/efficient treatment for me, even when I felt completely powerless and incapable of doing *anything*. Completely taken over by my eating disorder, I learned that I could always be honest. **This was something I could always do, no matter how much I was struggling and no matter how bad I felt,** and doing so did nothing but benefit me greatly. In this way, I started to take charge of my life. I started to do what I needed to do to protect myself against my eating disorder. My eating disorder was no longer my ally. (Not that it ever was, although I used to think it was.) My eating disorder was my enemy. It wanted to kill me and would not quit until it did. I began to ask for help to save myself.

Later on in recovery, by being honest, day in and day out, I was able to build myself back from relapse several times. With more time and practice, I was able to later catch myself mid-relapse, and eventually build back from slips or stop myself from engaging in any.

Eventually I reached a point where I would use honesty as a tool for self-awareness. Being honest about everything gave me the capacity to have much more insight into my own strengths and flaws, what triggered me and what helped me move forward in recovery, to notice signs where I was at risk of turning to my eating disorder—just having thoughts. Today, I use honesty as a form of self-awareness, to keep myself on track and protected against my eating disorder.

Remember, *eating disorders cannot thrive in honesty.* Take the power back by stripping your illness of its environment in where it thrives—secrecy.

Note: It is important to be honest both when you are doing well and when you are struggling. **Do not wait to be honest until things reach a crisis point.** *People cannot help you in the way that you need if they do not know how you are really doing.* No one is a mind reader. The sooner you are honest, the sooner you can put a stop to the eating disorder if you are struggling (halt a relapse), and the better off you will be in your recovery by being honest and staying accountable. Make it a habit to practice honesty every day. In this way, when things get difficult, it will be that much easier to be honest once it is already a habit.

Tip: If you find it hard to communicate face-to-face with your team, calling your therapist, writing them an e-mail, or sending them a text message can all be effective alternatives. When I was having a difficult time being honest with my therapist, I talked with her and made an agreement that I could e-mail her when I was struggling. I would write her an e-mail and send it to her immediately—that way, I had no way of "backing out" or being dishonest with her the next time I spoke with her.

It was also a way for me to reach out at any point—without feeling the need to wait to see her or call her at an appropriate time. By e-mailing her, I left it up to her to respond to me. Either way, I was being honest and saying what I needed to say in the moment.

Talk to your therapist and/or team to figure out a way where you can stay accountable and be 100 percent honest. Figure out what works best for you. Practice honesty. Right now. Today and every day. This continues to be one of my most useful tools in eating disorder recovery. Honesty. One hundred percent. Always.

"Hiding your problem only intensifies it. Problems grow in the dark and only become bigger and bigger, but when exposed to the light of truth, they shrink. You are only as sick as your secrets. So take off your mask, stop pretending you're perfect, and walk into freedom."
—Purpose Driven Life Book

2 | Using Your Voice (Reaching Out)

*Use your voice to communicate
how much you are hurting, not your body.*

It doesn't matter if you are just beginning your path of recovery, if you have been in treatment for years, or if you have yet to embark on your journey. Asking for help is *never* a sign of weakness. It takes a lot of courage and strength to do so. Asking for help exemplifies your will and dedication toward your recovery.

Eating disorders are **real illnesses**. They require professional treatment like any other serious illness. You have no reason to feel ashamed, selfish, or embarrassed when asking for the help you deserve and need. By reaching out, you are taking action. You are actively participating in your recovery. You are separating yourself from your eating disorder. You are using your voice (instead of your eating disorder's voice) by attending to your needs (and not your eating disorder's needs).

How do I reach out?

- If you are at a point where you feel like you have no support in place, there are many resources available. Check out the "Resources" section at the end of this book for hotline numbers and information on where you can get support *right now*.

- If you already have a treatment team, and you're in a place where you are struggling, reach out to someone on your team. Call your therapist, psychiatrist, or nutritionist. Be honest and reach out to a trusted family member or friend.
- Remember that there are many ways to reach out. If you cannot call someone, e-mailing them or sending them a text message are other options. If you still cannot get ahold of anyone, you can get immediate support by calling a free hotline or speaking with someone online, or reaching out to a trusted* online support network or group. See "Resources" for more information.

No matter where you are in recovery, you *deserve* to get the help you need, and there *is* help available. If you are having a hard time finding treatment options, don't give up. Keep looking. Ask. Call treatment centers and ask about payment/scholarship options. Call a hotline; ask a therapist . . .

Most importantly, do not isolate and struggle in silence. You never need to walk alone.

Are you struggling right now?

Be honest and *reach out right now*. Do not wait until things reach a crisis point to be honest and reach out for help. You *need* to be honest with your support team. It is a slippery and dangerous downward slope once your eating disorder starts taking over. Don't let it. If you feel like you cannot fight back and you need MORE support than you already have in place, you need to reach out. If you are struggling but not at a crisis point, you *still* need to reach out right now. Do not wait. Your life cannot wait. You do not deserve to wait. Remember, little things add up in recovery. If you are struggling it is important to get support. You deserve to get support.

If you have a treatment team, support group, or network of people who support you in your recovery, reach out to someone. If you don't, there are resources where you can reach out to right now. (See "Resources.")

Are you a student?

When I first accepted that I needed help to recover, I didn't know where to begin. The first thing I did (since I began recovery when I was college) was to go to my college counseling center. I found it to be *very* helpful. The counselors I met were very understanding and supportive. Not only did they set me up to meet with a counselor several times a week, they immediately put me in contact with a therapist specialized in eating disorders, a psychiatrist, and an eating disorder support group in my area. This group of brave women provided me so much support, hope, and understanding that only others facing similar struggles could provide.

Later on in my recovery, I would meet with a counselor at my school once a week (aside from my regular therapy appointments). I continued to find it helpful to have such easily accessible support at school. A place where I could be honest. If you are a student, you may want to check out your counseling center to determine counseling services available. They are often available for students on campus with little or no cost at all.

I remember feeling ashamed when I first made my way to the counseling center at school. Don't be. They are there for a reason. Many students talk with counselors, whether they are struggling with an eating disorder or something entirely different. If you are a student, you have resources available for you on campus. Use them.

"One thing that all people have in common . . . is that none of us are bulletproof. Asking for help is not a sign that you are weak. It's something that takes courage. And there is no one who is going to think you are any less of a person because you need some support. We all need support. But it takes strength to be able to ask for it."
—Author unknown

3

Follow Your Recovery
Plan 100 Percent

"No matter what."

You cannot afford to not take your medicine—to "cheat" your recovery plan

I remember when I began eating regular meals again. After leaving residential treatment and going back home, I would constantly compare what everyone was eating to what I was eating. *What is this person eating, what is that person eating, how much did they serve themselves, what are they eating, how much are they eating, did they eat more than me, did they eat less than me, did they finish everything on their plate* . . .

Not only was this incredibly *exhausting* mentally, but it made no sense for my recovery. All it did was exhaust me, increase my anxiety, make me hold irrational grudges against people, and waste time ruminating over negative thoughts. It took me out of the present moment, instead of focusing on enjoying my food and the company of the wonderful people around me.

You cannot afford to cheat on your meal plan—or any part of your recovery plan* if you want to recover. Doing so will only keep you stuck in your eating disorder. It can lead dangerously back to relapse even if you are at a currently stable position. *You have to always bear in mind that you are in recovery from a life-threatening illness.* If you are eating with a family member or friend who decides to not finish their meal, it is no excuse for you to not follow your meal plan. People who do not have eating disorders can afford to veer off of a consistent meal plan from time to time (not that it is healthy to do so, because it isn't). But they can *afford* to do so.

It's as if a person in recovery from alcoholism goes out to dinner with friends. Let's say the person's friends order wine for the table. The people who do not struggle with alcohol dependency can afford to have a glass of wine with their dinner. Their life and well-being are not at stake if they have a glass of wine. Similarly, think of a person who has diabetes. If they go out to have ice cream with a friend of theirs who does not have diabetes, is it fair to say that the person with diabetes does not have to monitor their insulin? Or can they eat their ice cream just like their friend will without taking any necessary precautions? Since their friend does not have to do so, then they wouldn't have to as well. Right?

Of course not. Just like a person with diabetes has to take their insulin (or their medicine), a person with an eating disorder needs to take their medicine. And for people with eating disorders, **food is their medicine.** Other things can help, but you cannot and will not recover if you do not eat, and eat accordingly to your nutritional needs. Remember, if you cheat on your recovery plan, you are only hurting yourself.

*When I talk about your recovery plan, I am not only referring to your meal plan. I am referring to any part of your treatment plan outlinesd to you by a team of professionals: your meal plan, exercise limitations, prescribed medications, and follow up appointments. *Everything that constitutes your treatment plan.* Everything "prescribed" to you by your treatment team.

Natalie Frost, the first therapist I worked with in recovery would constantly emphasize this to me. I would come up with excuse after excuse as to why I hadn't followed my meal plan. *I didn't have time to eat, I was super busy with classes, I forgot, I didn't like the food that was available, etc.* Natalie would say to me, time and time again:

"It is your responsibility to take care of yourself no matter what circumstances you are in." After stabilizing a bit only to relapse again, I finally began listening and *doing* what it is that she was telling me to do. I stopped making excuses, and I began following my recovery plan despite anything else—whether or not I felt like doing so, whether I felt like I had the time to do so or not. *No matter what.*

Taking care of yourself means feeding yourself adequately (following your meal plan), sticking to exercise limits, going to all of your appointments. It means following your recovery plan 100 percent, no excuses. I wasted valuable time in recovery attempting to "recover" while at the same time restricting on my recovery plan. I thought that if I followed my meal plan *mostly,* if I ate *almost everything* on my meal plan, if I exercised *just a little bit more* than I was supposed to, then I would be fine. I was wrong. **Cheating on my recovery plan—restricting on it even the tiniest bit, ALWAYS led me to relapse.** So what did I do? I started following my recovery plan 100 percent. I realized that if I wanted to recover 100 percent, then I would have to follow recovery 100 percent. How could I expect to be completely free of my illness if I was still holding on to parts of it? *You get out of treatment what you put into it.*

I began doing what I needed to do. I stopped making excuses and started finding solutions. If I knew I had a busy day ahead of me, I would wake up 15 minutes earlier than usual and pack my meals ahead of time. I would plan my class and work schedule around mealtimes (I even spoke with my supervisor at work once about *needing* to have a lunch break due to a medical condition). I didn't take on jobs that prohibited meals or snacks during shifts. I took recovery seriously. It became my number-one priority.

You may have noticed that I emphasize *no matter what* when it comes to following through in your recovery.

Some friends from treatment and I came up with a motto to live by in recovery: "No matter what." You can apply it to everything in recovery. We would use the motto when writing to each other about our accomplishments in recovery or goals for that day, week, or month. It really helped me to set goals for the week. You don't have to say, "I will never relapse no matter what" or set unrealistic goals that can frustrate you if you don't accomplish them. Start out small. Remember, the key here is progress, not perfection. Break it down to daily goals, then weekly, monthly, and so forth.

Here are some examples of daily goals that we would set for ourselves:

Today, I will follow my meal plan <u>no matter what</u>.
I will be honest with my therapist today <u>no matter what</u>.
I will practice healthy coping skills instead of turning to my eating disorder tonight <u>no matter what</u>.
I will call a friend and ask for support today <u>no matter what</u>.

And then, weekly goals such as:
I will go to all of my appointments this week <u>no matter what</u>.
I will not restrict any meals today <u>no matter what</u>.

If you fall short of your goal, don't beat yourself up. Do the next best thing for your recovery. Remember, you can choose to get back on track at any given moment. Also, don't make it an option to *not* follow your meal plan. When you do that, it becomes that much easier—there is no room for arguing in your head—going back and forth with your eating disorder—should you hesitate or not want to follow it.

Do what you need to do. Your treatment team will work with you to create a "recipe for success" (recovery plan). But it is up to you to follow it. You decide with each decision where you want to go toward—illness or freedom. And the best part about this? You can always begin again if you happen to slip up. But why wait? Choose recovery *right now*.

4

Slips

Slips happen. It's okay. Keep going.

This is not an easy road to recovery. Slips happen. They don't mean that you are back to square one. A slip is just a slip, and it can be overcome by getting back on the right path.

Jenni Schaefer, author and spokesperson of the National Eating Disorders Association (NEDA), writes in her bestselling book, *Life Without Ed:* "A relapse is like a leak in the roof. We do not plan for it. Sometimes we do not know why it started. But we must take care of it as soon as possible. We must make it a priority. Just think about it. If water were dripping steadily from your ceiling onto your leather sofa, you would not sit around and wallow in sadness for a while over the fact that your sofa was getting ruined. No, you would take action quickly. Move the sofa; patch the roof. And that is just what has to be done with relapse" (Schaefer J. *Life Without Ed.* New York, NY: McGraw-Hill).

* Note: When Jenni talks about relapse she is referring to *any* slip or reverting to an eating disorder behavior.

So, how do you "patch up the roof" when you have a slip? By **choosing the next best thing** for your recovery. In my opinion, the best part about recovery is that you can choose to get back on track at any given moment.

You are not "starting over" if you fall back into an eating disorder behavior. A friend of mine, Kathy, who recovered from anorexia and bulimia, states this concept wonderfully: "I know it's the popular way of conceptualizing recovery but I don't think it is necessary to 'start over' every time you slip. It doesn't do justice to the days that you had in recovery. Just remember that you know what recovery feels like, and therefore, you can keep doing it. There are ups and downs in all of life—it's about making the ups more frequent than the downs and getting back on track as soon as you can."

Restricting

I struggled mainly with restriction when I was sick. I am not going to go into details about my own struggles, as I don't find it necessary or helpful in any way to explain details which can be triggering or counterproductive to people in recovery. It doesn't matter if you restrict a little or a lot; in recovery, you cannot restrict *at all*.

I put together a list with some of my friends that includes some of the *many* reasons to *never* restrict:
- You set yourself up to binge later.
- Detrimental for your health, slows down your metabolism.
- Restricting causes you to think about food all day.
- Leads to isolation.
- Depletes muscle.
- Perpetuates feelings of guilt.
- Treatment is hard; you set yourself up to have to do it again.
- Restricting is a way to avoid feelings, good and bad.
- INCREASES anxiety as the bout shifts into fight-or-flight survival mode.
- Medication cannot work if you restrict.
- Shifts in mood; easy to feel depressed.
- Leads to isolation.
- Restricts you physically as you have less energy.
- Restricting is a way to avoid feelings, good and bad.
- Hunger causes insomnia.

- Medical complications, such as low blood sugar, orthostatic hypotension, heart arrhythmias, electrolyte imbalances . . . to name a few.
- Almost every eating disorder starts with a diet. The first three letters in diet spell DIE.
- Other long-term health problems, such as with your heart, brain function, eyesight, and dental.
- Loss of concentration.
- Anorexia has a higher suicide rate than depression.
- *Because food is fucking delicious.* (Couldn't help but agree with this one 100 percent!)
- Starving increases stress hormones, leading to irritation and freak-outs!
- Constant twitches and tics from hypokalemia and other vitamin deficiencies.
- *It's never enough. The lower you go in calories and pounds, the lower you want to go. There is no bottom—other than rock bottom or death.*

Cognitive changes, like difficulty concentrating and making decisions, are common. I can't describe the *frustration* and *impotency* I felt when I *could not concentrate.* Not only was I not able to get anything done in school (something that frustrated me greatly because I hadn't had any difficulty with school in my childhood), but I loved writing and suddenly found myself staring at a blank sheet of paper for hours, only to jot down a few incongruent words attempting to form a sentence. I also remember not being able to read over a few sentences in one sitting. *The words simply would not sink in,* despite rereading the same page again and again. Not being able to keep a conversation going felt very debilitating as well. I could not keep up with what people were saying. It was as if the person in front of me started suddenly talking in some alien language after the first few words. As hard as I tried to focus on what they were saying, their words did not make sense to me. I couldn't make sense of what they were saying. And if they said something that I could remember in that moment, I would forget it a few minutes later.

(What did she tell me her name was? What did she tell me she was going to do today?) This was both *perplexing and terrifying to me.*

In addition to these debilitating symptoms, I suffered from insomnia often. Sleep disturbance is common if you are restricting. Emotional instability, apathy, and depression are also common. Check, check, check. Anxiety. Check. Amenorrhea, hypotension, heart irregularities, reduced body temperature which makes you feel cold all the time, hair loss, growth of lanugo hair (which your body produces in order to "protect itself" and keep itself from freezing) are also serious and common symptoms in anorexia. Check.

Once again, these are only *some* of the countless symptoms that accompany anorexia. And they are some of the *many* reasons why you should never restrict. Your body will not survive on x amount of calories simply because your eating disorder tries to convince you that it can.

Fighting for Your Life: Survival Mode

When your body expends more calories than it consumes, it goes into starvation mode. "In order to survive, what, to the mind may be a long period of time without nutrients, the body does the most efficient thing. The body begins to lose fat and muscle mass and immediately breaks these down for energy. The body breaking down its own muscles and other tissues in order to salvage what energy it can in order to keep vital organs running is known as catabolysis.

"If restriction continues, stomach atrophy occurs, which is why people no longer feel hunger or thirst cues. It is easy to become dehydrated at this point.

"When you are sick with an eating disorder, losing hunger cues may feel like a personal triumph. In reality, this is the beginning of atrophy, or wasting away of many of their bodily tissues" ("Eating Disorders Still Claiming Lives").

According to Dr. Alfredo Hatchett, specialist in adolescent medicine and professor in addictions treatment, "The consequences of severe anorexia include malnutrition which, in extreme cases, causes multiple organ failure." Depriving your body of vital nutrients and fluids over a period of time affects all bodily systems. No organ is spared. The main causes of death by anorexia include multiple organ failure and cardiac arrest.

Aside from the numerous health risks associated with restricting, it also perpetuates bingeing, putting you at risk to engage in other eating disorder behaviors. Restricting food increases food thoughts, cravings, and sets you up for bingeing. In order to stop bingeing, you need to stop restricting. I will talk more about that in a moment.

Your hunger signals will come back and your body will adjust (the body really is miraculous at repairing itself), but you must feed it well. Also, there was a lot of work I could not do in recovery until I had reached a medically stable weight range. I didn't realize how much being underweight affected me mentally and emotionally besides physically.

Many of the changes that took place I wasn't even aware of until I was stabilized physically again. I could feel the differences. I felt great. I had forgotten how it felt to feel good, to be healthy, to have energy, to think clearly, to be able to read and understand and keep a conversation going. I remember when I started to feel hunger signals again. Obsessive food thoughts disappeared . . . It really is amazing.

It's funny because I remember reading testimonials from eating disorder survivors and rolling my eyes as I read about a seemingly "euphoric" state of recovery which I could only *imagine,* yet never believe to be true for *me.* Now I can reiterate other survivors' words. *Full freedom from an eating disorder is possible.* And, YES—it really *is* amazing. It is better than I could have ever imagined. To answer a question I asked myself years ago, and a question many of you might have, "Is recovery really worth it?" The answer is *yes,* every single part of recovery is worth it.

Bingeing

I struggled with bingeing in the latter years of my illness. After restricting on food for so long, I started experiencing intense cravings which led me to uncontrollable eating episodes. This is not uncommon. I know a lot of people who, after restricting for a period of time, began struggling with bingeing. (Note: bingeing isn't always precipitated by restriction.) In my case, however, this led to dangerous binge-starve-binge-starve- cycles, and it opened to door to bulimia for me. Why is this?

When your body goes into starvation mode, your mind becomes bombarded with food thoughts, preoccupations regarding food, intense cravings, and possibly dreams about food. There have been numerous investigations done on this subject. In the Minnesota studies (Keys et al. 1950), "when normal young men were placed on semistarvation diets for a number of months, they developed many food-related symptoms that are seen in people with anorexia. These included a great preoccupation with food, food-related thoughts and dreams (to the point where many of them collected recipes, enjoyed feeding others, and some wanted to become chefs) and intense hunger." Some of the men developed bulimic episodes (Garfinkel, P., Kasplan S. A., 1985).

Similarly, if your brain and body are missing essential nutrients, it is normal for you to begin experiencing cravings and constant thoughts regarding food.

"The brain is an organ that cannot store glycogen or oxygen on its own (without food). When nutrition deficiency occurs, the brain does have enough glycogen to function normally. This causes anxiety, sleeps disorders, cognitive impairment such as decision making and concentration and increased thoughts regarding food," says Dr. Hatchett.

If you restrict your food intake, even just a little, you are setting yourself up to binge. Binges can be seen as mechanisms utilized to fill emotional or physical gaps. That being said, binges can occur whether restriction has taken place or not. According to the NHS, "episodes of binge eating often alternate with periods where the person severely cuts down on the amount of food they eat, which can make the problem worse" (binge eating). Once again, bingeing does not need to be precipitated by restriction in order to occur. Binge eating disorder includes episodes of bingeing, similar to those in bulimia. But a huge way to prevent binges (filling the physical gap) is by following a regular eating schedule (set up by a RD or nutritionist specialized in eating disorders).

"Binge eating usually takes place in private, with the person feeling that they have no control over their eating. They will often have feelings of guilt or disgust after binge eating. These feelings highlight underlying psychological issues, such as low self-esteem and lack of confidence, depression, and anxiety. These feelings can be made worse over time while the person is still binge eating." The only way I was finally able to stop bingeing and experiencing cravings was to follow my meal plan—completely. Any "cheating" of food on my part only led to cravings, which, most of the time, turned into a slip or relapse. *Follow your recovery plan 100 percent.*

Reasons to not binge:
- Increases anxiety, most often heightening urges to purge, thus perpetuating the binge—Purge-Restrict cycle, a violent attack on the body
- Temporarily "numbs" disturbing feelings . . . not permanently
- Slows your metabolism
- Causes bloating
- Causes lethargy
- Bingeing can lead to purging which is really bad for your heart, teeth, organs, skin, esophagus, etc.
- Causes feelings of immense guilt and shame (extremely unpleasant)
- Immense physical discomfort and pain
- Financial anxiety—It is expensive to binge and even more expensive to pay for treatment to manage the behavior.

Binge eating disorder can cause high blood pressure, high cholesterol levels, heart disease due to elevated triglyceride levels, type

2 diabetes, mellitus, and gallbladder disease ("Get the Facts on Eating Disorders"). It is not uncommon for people with **any eating disorder** to struggle with bingeing. I know the uncomfortable feeling and thoughts of guilt and shame that arise after a binge. Remember that one day of bingeing or overeating in the grand scheme is not going to matter. It's when that day turns into may or the aftermath of what you do because of that binge . It's the restricting and other behaviors that you do to try to compensate that will affect your weight and metabolism.

I read a message which I found helpful when I was struggling:

If you binge . . . forgive yourself . . . and then continue eating your meal plan—regardless of how much/what you consumed by bingeing. Your body will adjust itself. It's pretty brilliant. But restricting will keep setting you up to binge.

Tips to prevent bingeing:
- Stick to a meal plan which meets your nutritional needs for where you are at (under the advice of a nutritionist or clinician). In this way, the meal plan can ensure that all biological reasons for bingeing are reduced.
- If you are not following a meal plan, then you may want to examine whether you are getting enough on a daily basis. This may be a reason for the binge.
- Do not be around trigger foods and/or buy foods in individual portions.
- Journal the process coming up to a binge (stress trigger, then contemplation, then deciding on and executing your binge). You need to stop the process before the urge to binge gets uncontrollable.
- Plan activities, preferably with someone, at your greatest risk time.
- Find better and more effective ways to deal with stress, anxiety, and other difficult emotions. Pull out a list of coping skills you can turn to in a moment of "urges." (See *"Coping Skills"* at the end of this book for a list of skills.)

- Have an "emergency plan" in place (this goes for all ED symptoms). See next page.

Purging

Severe health consequences occur as a result of purging methods—esophagus problems, esophagus rupture, and cardiac problems. Laxatives can cause permanent colon problems, and diuretics can lead to renal problems. According to the National Eating Disorders Association, "the recurrent binge-and-purge cycles of bulimia can affect the entire digestive system and can lead to electrolyte and chemical imbalances in the body that affect the heart and other major organ functions" ("Get The Facts On Eating Disorders").

Some of the health consequences associated with purging include:
- Tooth decay
- Inflammation and/or esophagus rupture
- Electrolyte imbalances (these can lead to cardiac abnormalities and death)
- Chronic constipation and irregular bowel movements
- Pancreatitis
- Peptic ulcers

Have an Emergency Plan in Place
If you have the urge to binge/purge/restrict, etc.*
A list of coping skills you can turn to

I love the idea that Jenni Schaefer suggests in her book *Life Without Ed*. When she was in recovery, Jenni's therapist suggested that she make an "Emergency 911 Card" that included relapse-prevention tips. Jenni made a card small enough so that she could carry it with her wherever she went. One side of the card included a list of phone numbers of people on her support team, and the other side included a list of what has really worked in the past in preventing a relapse (Schaefer J., *Life Without Ed*. New York, NY: McGraw-Hill).

If you decide to make a coping list or card for yourself (I did it and found it very helpful), check out the "Coping Skills" section at the end of this book for over a hundred different ideas that may work for you. Remember, what works for one person might not work for you. Go through the list, try some out, and figure out what works best for you.

This is what I put on my 911 card:

1. Move energy (push as hard as you can against a wall)—great to relieve tension
2. Take a walk—get out of the house; get some fresh air
3. PHONE/CALL FOR SUPPORT (DO NOT HESITATE)
4. Look up eating disorders support groups online to have support no matter where you are (there are many professional, moderated groups that exist—I can't emphasize how helpful these were to me!)

AFTER A SLIP:

Remember: *You're okay.*

It's okay to have a slip in a week. Or two or three or more. It's *okay*. You are not back at square one. Just make the next best choice right now for your recovery and keep moving forward.

1. Stay safe. *What can you do **right now** to avoid falling into further ED behaviors?*
2. *Call someone on your support network, practice healthy coping skills that work best for you, use your 911 list/card.*
3. Choose the next best thing for your recovery.

Tip: Stay away from the scale and remember, you are NOT a number!

STOPPING yourself from engaging in eating disorder behaviors . . .

Toward the latter years of my eating disorder, I fell into a dangerous and torturous cycle of restricting, bingeing, and purging. When I was struggling, I would often think that struggling with one behavior *automatically meant I would have to "fix" my mistake with another eating disorder behavior.* If I binged, I would feel overwhelmed with guilt and anxiety, and my automatic thought in that moment would be something like, *"Now I have to purge or restrict to make up for all the food I just consumed."*

Little did I see the irrationality wanting to "fix" an eating disorder behavior with another eating disorder behavior. It was as if I had broken my foot and expected to heal it by breaking my entire leg. (It sounds crazy, but they are both just as illogical.) In order to break this self-defeating cycle, I first had to learn to separate one behavior from another.

In the beginning, this is what I did. In the beginning, this is what I did. Even if I couldn't "control" or overcome urges and repeatedly fell into a continuous negative cycle, I realized that each behavior was a behavior on its own. It was its own behavior; and it was preceded by a decision. *My decision.*

I had to recognize that I **made the decision** whether or not to engage in a behavior.

I began to accept responsibility. Even if I did struggle, I had to accept that I *did* have a choice in engaging in an eating disorder behavior, and that when I did struggle, I *had* made the decision to follow through with the ED behaviors.

The point here is not to self-sabotage and blame yourself for struggling. Remember, I said that there is a difference between something being your fault and something being your responsibility. Blaming yourself will not take you anywhere positive. Taking responsibility while being kind to yourself throughout the process begins to give you your power back.

Also, struggling with one behavior would first make me feel miserable and guilty, like I had "failed." This way of thinking detonated the destructive ED cycle, making it feel almost "automatic" for me to keep engaging in ED behaviors.

As I began to take power back and 1) *separate* behaviors and 2) accept that I *could*, in fact, choose to engage in a behavior (or not) (at any time), then I began to be able to stop myself—to choose—recovery over my eating disorder.

If I had just binged:

- No, it did not feel good to binge. But here I was, faced with a decision:
    - » Choose the next best thing and cope healthily

      OR
    - » Purge or restrict, thus, feel worse and fall further and further into the ED cycle

In order to reach a solid state of recovery I had to learn to *STOP* myself, to separate one behavior from another. This was especially challenging in the beginning. If I binged, I HAD to learn to sit with myself with the uncomfortable emotions and pain that I experienced physically and mentally. I felt miserable. I felt sick to my stomach. I felt a million different emotions all at once. And yet—the uncomfortable feelings passed. The stomach pain went away. In the end, by refusing to engage in a second behavior just because I had engaged in one, *I actually felt better*. I felt *accomplished*. I started to feel in charge of myself and my life, not controlled by an illness that only caused me misery. This took awhile, of course. The first few times I stopped myself halfway through a slip, I didn't feel accomplished or proud of myself in any way at all. I felt gross and like a failure. Part of me felt like I was a failure if I didn't "go through" with the behavior. But in the back of my mind, I *knew* it was the right thing to do. I had to do what I knew was the right thing to do, even if I didn't feel good about it (for a long time). Eventually, I began to feel good about doing the right thing. And later it became automatic, part of my lifestyle.

When I say that the best part about recovery is that you can choose to get back on track at any given moment, I really do mean that you can get back on track *at any moment*. Choosing the next best thing for your recovery can start as soon as *this moment*. Right now. If you are purging, stop yourself and go outside, call a friend to distract you, or immediately walk away from where you are. If you are bingeing, you can choose to stop and call a friend to let out your frustration or whatever it is you are feeling. You can choose, at any time to engage in healthy coping skills rather than revert to eating disorder behaviors.

You hold your own key to success—the power of *choice*. Not all people who struggle with a life-threatening illness have the choice to recover. Think of this as a blessing. It is. You do have the choice to recover. And you can. One choice at a time.

Right now, what do you choose?

Remember that slips will happen; they are a part of this nonlinear path of recovery.

When you have a slip:
1. Stay safe. This is where coping skills and 911 cards come into play.
2. Practice healthy coping skills/self-care.
3. Be gentle with yourself. Remember that slips will happen; they are a part of the recovery process.
4. Try to identify your triggers. Can you pinpoint what was going on when you engaged in the behavior? What uncomfortable or painful feelings were you experiencing or trying to avoid? It's important to examine this to prevent slips. Use this information to note your triggers and discuss this information with your therapist.

5

Relapse

Falling is not failing.

Breaking the fall

Relapse is not uncommon in recovery. Keep in mind that recovery is a *process*, with its ups and downs. It is not linear. If you find yourself relapsing, **reach out for help immediately.** It might not *feel* easy to reach out for help in the moment. The reality is that you *can* keep yourself from spiraling. The sooner you get support, the sooner you get back on track. Reaching out for help during relapse involves what was previously outlined—being *100 percent honest at all times, using your voice to ask for help—and choosing the next best thing for your recovery.*

Relapse just means you still have something you need to work on.

The following passage is an excerpt from Laurie Glass, author of *Journey to Freedom from Eating Disorders*, anorexia survivor, and certified clinician counselor:

Relapses in eating disorder recovery are a very common part of the recovery process. This journey is filled with stops and starts; steps forward and steps backward; renewed motivation and giving into the eating disorder; hope and hopelessness; falls and victories. One may forge ahead for a time, then become ambivalent and give only reserved efforts. After a period of success, one may lose that initial resolve and get stuck or even relapse. It's no wonder we get discouraged, question why we try, and sometimes even give up.

Relapses in eating disorder recovery may be overwhelming, but I don't want this article to sound negative. I just describe recovery in this fashion to assure you that if you've experienced **relapses in eating disorder recovery,** you are not alone. Please be patient with yourself and understand that what you're going through is very common. Eating disorders are complicated so it only stands to reason that breaking free of them is a difficult and sometimes a perplexing process.

Relapses in eating disorder recovery are something I've experienced myself, so I comprehend how difficult the steps backward and even the falls can be for a person. I basically went from halfhearted efforts to giving into the eating disorder during much of the time I was anorexic. Breaking free of the life of self-destruction seemed impossible to me, and I didn't want to go to all of that hard work only to experience **relapses in eating disorder recovery** again. I realize it's different for everyone, but I'll just say that for me, it was the determination to recover like I hadn't had before, as well as leaning on God like I hadn't before that made recovery possible.

So, stops and starts, victories and relapses—what can be done? Here are some things to keep in mind to help you work through the challenging times.

1. Give yourself permission to have a less-than-perfect recovery experience. It's okay to struggle and even to fall sometimes.
2. As frustrating as it can be, realize that the back-and-forth thinking is just part of the process. Going from wanting to recover to not wanting to recover is normal. If you weren't trying at all, you wouldn't be frustrated, so give yourself a pat on the back for trying.
3. Learn from the steps backward, the falls, and the relapses. Examine what caused them and use those insights to do what you can to prevent them from happening again. You can then come out of these experiences stronger and more prepared for upcoming challenges.

4. Focus on the steps forward in your recovery. Concentrate on the positive things you've done.
5. Do your best not to beat yourself up when you get stuck or even when you step backward. Recovering from your eating disorder is one of the most, if not the most, difficult things you will ever do. Give yourself credit for the courage to try.
6. Remember that your eating disorder didn't appear overnight, and it won't go away easily. Give yourself time to address the complicated issues that make up an eating disorder.
7. Be patient with yourself; give you insights about what happened, and to strengthen you to face upcoming challenges .

Don't be surprised if you experience some **relapses in eating disorder recovery.** Learn what you can from them and come out stronger. If you are religious and have faith, let God help you get back on track. Remember that He wants only the best for you so you can trust Him with your recovery concerns. Be gentle with yourself and celebrate your victories.

I wrote the following message to a friend when she was struggling. It was the first time I had been able to "catch myself" during a relapse and build back from it to a stable place:

*I was relapsing badly for several weeks. I was already calling treatment centers. I was very desperate and felt **trapped** in the eating disorder cycle. I am saying this to let you know that I was just there where you are now. I know you must feel like it's impossible to "get out," but, really, all you have to do is make that choice to get back on the recovery track. And stay on it no matter what. This doesn't mean you won't have slips. It just means that, if you fall into a behavior, you will do **the next best thing** for your recovery—NOT say "screw it" and give into the eating disorder more. Slips happen, but it does not mean a relapse unless you give your eating disorder that power again and again.*

Even if you do happen to relapse (which happened to me several times throughout my recovery), you can *always* choose to get back on track. In order to do so, I recommend that you set up a plan, like a "how-to get back on track," "Back to basics." (I also recommend setting up a Relapse Prevention Plan with your treatment team, which I will talk about in more detail later in this book.)

So if you find that you are relapsing or feeling like you are back at square one, here is the plan that worked for me to get back on track. The trick is—start *right now*!

6

Back to Basics

Recovery after a slip or relapse

1. Follow your recovery plan 100 percent.
   (This includes following *all* parts of your treatment plan 100 percent. Meal plan, exercise restriction or limitation, keeping up with *all* of your appointments, etc.)

2. If you slip, it's *okay*. Breathe and **do the next best thing** for your recovery.
   This is *difficult*, I know. If you binge for example, you are going to have to eat your next meal normally, and continue on with your meal plan. This is sticking to recovery. This is doing the next best thing.

3. Keep choosing recovery no matter what.
   *** Recovery takes practice. Be gentle with yourself and have patience. How long did you engage in your eating disorder? It has become a coping mechanism, a habit. By choosing recovery again and again and again and *again*, you will make recovery a habit. You will practice healthy coping skills, and learn more and more along the way. (See "Coping Skills" section.) Soon enough, engaging in healthy coping skills won't be so *difficult, foreign,* and *scary*. Before you know it, choosing

healthily will become acceptable, comfortable, and finally, enjoyable. What was once so "comfortable" (ED) will be so foreign and long behind you.

4. Use your resources.

   Recovery isn't easy, and you shouldn't have to do this alone. Having a solid support system was key for my recovery. And you don't have to have an entire football team cheering you on. One or two people who you can confide in and "go to" at all times can be more than enough.

   Always surround yourself with support, especially when you are having a hard time.

"Bicker with the bitch in your head who keeps telling you you're fat and weak, Shut up, you say; I'm busy, leave me alone. When she leaves you alone, there's a silence and a solitude that will take some getting used to. You will miss her sometimes. Bear in mind she's trying to kill you. Bear in mind you have a life to live."
—Marya Hornbacher

7

Treatment

"You survived the abuse. You can survive the recovery."
—*Olivia Benson*

There are several different treatment options available for people struggling with eating disorders. What works for one person might not work for another person. What worked for me might not work for you. My best advice would be to meet with a professional (a doctor or therapist specialized in eating disorders) to help guide you and choose what kind of treatment is best for you. Individual therapy, nutritional guidance, psychiatric/medical treatment, family therapy, and support group meetings often make up a complete program.

Jan Lockert, (eating disorder survivor, healthcare professional and Director of Admissions and Outreach at the River Centre Clinic for Eating Disorders in Toledo, Ohio), Tina Nowak (RN and Executive Director at Tapestry Treatment Center for Eating Disorders in Brevard, North Carolina), and Dr. Isabel Kuthy (Psychiatrist with years of experience working with people struggling with eating disorders) answer the following questions regarding treatment:

What are the different types of treatment available for people struggling with eating disorders?
Tina: There is acute inpatient treatment (usually in a hospital) for crisis stabilization. Typically, 4–12 days on a locked psychiatric unit.

Residential treatment is typically a free-standing facility that provides treatment 24 hours a day, 7 days a week. It can be locked or unlocked. Partial hospitalization (PHP) refers to a 4–6 hour program that runs 5 days a week that provides basic meal planning, meal support, individual therapy, etc. IOP (intensive outpatient treatment) is a 2-hour-a-day, 3-day-a-week supportive program that provides individual sessions and groups. Outpatient treatment includes individual sessions with a therapist, MD, or nutritionist.

Jan: The different levels of care often dictate the approaches, such as outpatient therapy (basically therapy to address coping skills and emotional distress). This level very seldom can offer the intensity and structure needed for someone to implement a recovery plan. Intensive outpatient (IOP) is also very limited in its ability to provide adequate structure, simply due to the duration of time a person spends in treatment and the demands for their personal accountability during independent time. Partial hospitalization (PHP) is often the most effective approach, along with residential, based on the needs of the person. Inpatient treatment is only necessary for those who are medically unstable to the point of needing 24-hour medical care and supervision. To determine a person's needs for treatment, an intensive, comprehensive assessment should be completed to evaluate all aspects of the person's needs. Medical testing should also be done, including an EKG , to establish medical status. The approaches used during treatment usually involve CBT, DBT (usually later on in the process), ACT, and a critical component is always a very structured meal plan, no matter what the presenting symptoms or diagnosis may be.

How do I know what level/kind of treatment is right for me?
Jan: An in-depth clinical assessment, including lab tests and an EKG, should be taken, and all should be evaluated by a skilled and experienced eating disorder clinician. The recommendation for the level of care can then be determined, based on this information.

How long does "recovery" take?

Jan: The process is very individualized, and all components of recovery can often take several years. Implementing self-care and emotional stability is a lifelong issue, but once the coping skills are "honed" and a person can identify that the eating disorder is no longer a problem, life in itself takes on a completely new dimension. I think it's important to remember that, like life, recovery isn't perfect, so don't expect it to be.

ED prognosis—what does it depend on?

Jan: The most important factor for staying well, especially initially after treatment, is to follow your specific aftercare plan, continue to see your outpatient therapist, and to not expect to be "normal" too quickly. Overall, the duration of illness, a person's age, past issues related to trauma, etc., personality traits, support system, etc., can all play a role in a person's prognosis.

Medical/Integrative approach for ED treatment: The importance of a complete/integrated treatment model (psychological, physical, emotional) to reach stability.

Jan: It's important to have some "framework" on which to base treatment, but a "cookie-cutter" approach can never be effective. Each person's presentation and needs are very specific, so their treatment plan should be just as individualized. In order to effectively provide treatment for a person with an eating disorder, a professional must be able to "think outside the box" and needs to consult with other professionals along the way. A team approach is essential.

Dr. Kuthy: In order for treatment to be successful, it needs to by multidisciplinary. In other words, treatment should be run by a team of professionals—not one person—which often includes a medical doctor, a psychiatrist, a therapist, a dietician, and in many cases, a social worker.

Co-occurring illnesses are not uncommon with eating disorders.
Dr. Kuthy: It isn't uncommon for co-occurring illnesses to exist along with eating disorders. Obsessive compulsive disorder, depression, anxiety disorders, and/or personality disorders are the most common. These illnesses are treated in conjunction since pharmaceutical medications are associated with various neurotransmitter pathways that are altered with these illnesses. Antidepressants, for example, can be successfully used to treat OCD and anxiety.

What do you recommend for patients who are "stable"? (Specific evaluations in order to avoid medical consequences that may often go unnoticed for years.)
Jan: It's important to keep in mind that any significant weight changes are not "normal." Seeing a therapist occasionally just to do a "self-check" could be an important preventive measure. If a person knows that they are facing a major life change or they have a tragedy in their life/family, it's good to consider going back to structured meal planning to secure that the emotional aspects aren't affecting one's eating behaviors. Also, having at least a yearly medical exam is an important component of self-care.

"Consistent nutritional evaluations are crucial," highlights Dr. Hatchett. "Blood tests that indicate chemical markers in the blood. And in order to avoid relapse, constantly work on self-esteem building."

How long?
"As long as it takes."

Advice for professionals treating eating disorders. (What is *key* to be aware of?)
Jan: CHANGE in a person's presentation, weight, mood, etc., are always important warning signs that a person may be struggling in some way. Also, any mention of wanting to stop or change the

treatment plan should be carefully examined and discussed with the patient.

"Cognitive issues," says Dr. Hatchett. "Always be aware of what the patient's thinking, where his or her thoughts are at. Also, from a professional standpoint—be open to work in collaboration/team. Eating disorders should not be treated by one health person only."

Treatment availability/Treatment options

What is the most "effective" type of treatment? What does it consist of?
Jan: Treatment should be "evidence-based" and approaches should be proven and backed by data and statistics. Individualized treatment plans should be developed with both the professional and the client, and all members of the treatment team.

Tina: Residential treatment with step-down to partial , IOP and OP, is the most effective to allow for a slow transition and support throughout the recovery process. In my opinion (as long as I was medically stable), this is the best way to go about treatment.

Are there scholarships/financial aid available for people seeking treatment?
Jan: This is an area where the options are limited, but some are available. There are a few resources available online to obtain this information.

Tina: For clients at Tapestry there are some scholarships available through various organizations. Clark Behavioral Health provides financing to clients who meet the criteria.

Tina: I would recommend that they do their research on the various types of programs and to really find one that supports them and provides a nurturing environment.

What drew you to work in this specific field? What advice could you give to someone who is just looking for treatment options/beginning their recovery?

Jan: My own personal struggles with an eating disorder and the recovery process is the core reason behind my decision to work in the field. I would advise someone to carefully seek out a clinician or a facility that specializes in eating disorders, has a long-standing history of providing evidence-based treatment, and, if possible, they know someone who has been through the process before. Also, staying open to treatment options, and accepting that they need help in order to manage their own recovery, is important. A person must be able and willing to give up the control for a while, in order to take back control in a healthy and manageable way. It's really OK to ask for help!

"An effective treatment program for eating disorders should address more than just your symptoms and destructive eating habits. It should also address the root causes of the problem—the emotional triggers that lead to disordered eating and your difficulty coping with stress, anxiety, fear, sadness, and other uncomfortable emotions ("Eating Disorder Treatment," Help Guide).

This is key. Many people are disappointed when they go to treatment where they are tube-fed or put on a weight-gain plan, stabilized medically, and then dismissed. Oftentimes, these treatments are **necessary in order to stabilize the patient medically. **However,** dismissing a patient from treatment once they reach a "target weight" can be (and usually is) detrimental **if they do not continue intensive treatment.** A person is not "cured" once they reach a certain weight.

Weight stabilization is key to recovery and is usually the first thing that needs to be done. Many treatment centers will not accept patients who are not medically stable. Once they are stabilized, however, the **real work** begins. Once stabilized, the patient can be stable enough to work through core issues in therapy.

When I first entered treatment for my eating disorder I was put on a weight gain meal plan. I remember constantly complaining (sorry,

Leslie!) about how uncomfortable I felt, how full I felt, and didn't understand why I had to eat so much in addition to drinking supplements throughout the day between meals.

"Vanessa, the supplements are nutrients for your *brain*," Nicole Fahy, therapist and eating disorder specialist, said to me in a session one day. "There is a lot of work you cannot even *begin* to do until your brain is adequately nourished."

This was true, and after hearing Nicole's words, I began to notice it for myself as my time in treatment went on. When I first arrived, I couldn't concentrate; I could barely make out what was being said to me. In no way could I have worked through *core issues* in therapy. Those first few weeks there are still a blur in my head. As I began eating regularly again, my body and brain began to repair themselves and function normally. I could finally *think*. My mind was no longer barraged by obsessive thoughts all day, the intensity of them died down, and I was much better able to cope. My anxiety decreased tremendously (starving puts your body in stress mode for survival), and, although recovery wasn't easy and I *was* uncomfortable with my weight in that moment, I *was* stable enough to be able to begin working on all of this, all of what would have previously pulled me back to my disorder—the issues that precipitated my eating disorder and perpetuated it.

I encourage you to speak with your treatment team/medical professional to guide you to what type of treatment you need. It is important that you find the treatment that properly addresses your specific needs in the moment. Since recovery is a constantly changing process, what you may need at one moment could be different from what you need at another, requiring different levels of treatment at different times. Depending on what you need, your doctor and/or eating disorder specialist may recommend outpatient treatment, day treatment, residential treatment, inpatient treatment, or hospitalization.

Beginning treatment

Are you beginning treatment for the first time?
Hang in there. I know it's hard. And confusing. And scary and sad

and painful, and so much more, all at once. But that is why you are there right now. Because you deserve this and need this support right now, and everyone there is there for you Things will get better. Just keep on keeping on. Remember that your life, your health, is what is most important, and that is what you are doing by being in treatment. Taking care of your health so you can live.

Focus on taking each day as it comes. Just one day, one meal, or one moment at a time. Things change so much in treatment, as they do in recovery, and as they do in life. Trust that you are exactly where you need to be right now. And when you leave treatment, you will be ready to leave.

Trust where you are, trust the process. Have faith and keep fighting.

Choose recovery, one day at a time. When you have a slip, it's okay. It doesn't mean you are back to the beginning. Just get up and keep moving forward. Do the next best thing for your recovery. Stay honest. And keep yourself surrounded by support.

You can do this! I am rooting for you. Remember that you are never alone.

You get out of treatment what you put into it.

I have repeated this a few times. Treatment is what you make of it. You get out of treatment what you put into it. If you put in 100 percent of your heart and effort into it and do the work (follow through treatment suggestions), you will get the most you can get out of it. Go to your appointments and do your best, participate in your recovery, and allow yourself to receive help. Allow yourself to be supported and receive the help you need and *deserve*.

Give this your ALL. You have nothing to lose and everything to gain. (With your eating disorder you have everything to lose—your life—and absolutely nothing to gain.) Fight your eating disorder and work hard 100 percent. **Listen to your treatment team;** they are there to help you overcome your eating disorder. Trust that they know what they are doing and do keep in mind that they are *on your side*, providing you the tools you need to overcome your eating disorder. This will be hard sometimes. When your eating disorder is fighting strongly against you, you may not feel like doing as your team suggests or may even not trust them.

When you are unsure of something or have doubts about your treatment, do not be afraid to speak up. It is ok to ask questions, to be informed about your recovery. This is your recovery. Putting yourself in the hands of professionals does not mean you are not an active participant in the process (you make the choices to follow through with their recommendations at the end of the day. And, you have every right to have your concerns addressed throughout the process).

As you develop a stronger sense of who you are without your eating disorder, and learn more and more tools to efficiently apply in your life, you will eventually apply these into your life without the help of a treatment team. Until you get there, trust them and believe in your treatment plan.

Going back to residential treatment

I went back to residential treatment more than once. When I went back the second time, I remember walking in to the clinical director's office with my head down, my eyes averted. I felt embarrassed, ashamed, and like I had failed miserably.

I sat down in an armchair without a word. She greeted me kindly and waited for a response.

A few minutes passed in silence.

"I'm a failure," I finally mumbled, sighing.

She looked at me with a genuine smile. "You are not a failure, Vanessa. You are very courageous, and I'm so proud of you for taking action and taking this brave step for your recovery," she said warmly. "You have nothing to be ashamed of—you should be proud of yourself."

I let out a sigh of relief. Surprisingly, I had similar positive/encouraging responses from everyone around me. I learned that relapsing (or going back to treatment) was not uncommon in recovery.

Taking action *immediately* when this happens, by getting back on track and/or reaching out for support, or admitting that you need *more* support than you have in place when you cannot get back on track is crucial. I remember she told me that my time in treatment wouldn't be the same as my first time. I wasn't "starting all over again," or "starting from zero."

I reflected on this and realized that I needed to be there in *that moment* and work on issues that were coming up for me *right then*. There was a reason I was there. Something wasn't working for me "outside" in the real world. There was something I needed to work on. *Right then, I had the opportunity to do so.*

Recovery isn't easy. It isn't straightforward. There is no how-to book—no 10-Step guideline that tells you how to recover, how long it will take, or how the therapeutic process will run its course. It is different for everyone. Recovery is messy. It is wonderful, terrible, exhausting, and rewarding—all at the same time. Ultimately, the gifts of recovery are spectacular. Recovery will save you and give you back the one thing that is truly meaningful in life—*you*. You will find, save, and rediscover yourself in the process, as well as the beauty surrounding you, and open your eyes to all of the opportunities life has to offer.

My eating disorder was the worst thing that ever happened to me. Recovery has been the best. It has given me back so much—my life. It hasn't come without a tremendous amount of hard work, patience, and dedication, but nothing that can be worth so much does. And you know what else is so great about recovery from an eating disorder? *That it's possible.* You CAN get there!

If you relapse, and you are able to go back to treatment, go. Do not hesitate. Take advantage of any help you can receive. If there is a support group in your area, go. I always see treatment as an *opportunity*, one in which you have room to heal, to learn, to thrive, to come back to life—stronger, wiser, more courageously and more insightful than you were before.

Since I played tennis for a long time, I often relate recovery to tennis. I like to think of treatment as a practice court, and the world outside of treatment as a tournament or a match. And the world outside of treatment as a "tournament" or match. You get to put what you learn in treatment into real-world practice.

Let's say you play a really bad tennis match. You can't focus, you miss all of your second serves, and you can't keep many balls in play. So what do you do? Quit the sport for good? No. You go back to the practice court; you practice every day on what you had trouble with in the tournament. And with practice, dedication, patience, and the guidance of your coaches and support from your peers, you begin to improve in those areas. You get more confident, and then another tournament comes along. You get another chance, and now with the practice and confidence under your belt, you have a new sense of security—you *know* you can do this. You are ready. Then comes your chance to leave the practice court and put your skills into play. And if you happen to not be ready? If you "fail miserably" again?

Another tournament will come along.

Just do your best.

Going back to residential treatment wasn't easy. At the moment I felt like a failure for going back, but deep down, *I knew it was what I needed*, so despite how miserable I felt, I went ahead and gave it my all. **Pro-recovery decisions like these were some of the best decisions I have made in my life.** I chose recovery over my eating disorder in times when my eating disorder was the strongest. (I did what I needed to do, despite how I felt.) In order to recover, recovery had to become my *number-one priority*. For example, if I was struggling and had to choose between going to treatment or staying in school, I chose treatment.

A part of me *hated* going back to treatment. *I hated knowing the work that I would need to do. The food I would need to eat, but especially—the feelings I knew I would need to feel. Feelings I wouldn't be able to numb, starve, purge, or run away from. Feelings I would have to feel.* The part of me that hated being in treatment was my *eating disorder*. The part of me that was scared, desperate for freedom, and willing to fight, was *me*.

So many people in recovery struggle and do not reach out for help, admit that they need it, or consider treatment. They suffer in silence. Being able to go to treatment was an opportunity and a blessing for me. Treatment saved my life.

If you are planning to go or are currently in treatment, whether it is outpatient, inpatient, partial treatment, or hospitalization, **take full advantage of it.** Look at treatment as an amazing opportunity to really step out of your comfort zone. To have space to simply breathe, to heal. To replenish and nourish your body, mind and soul. To work through underlying pain that only hold you back in your life. To reclaim your life as you fight your eating disorder and work towards the full, healthy life you deserve.

You have your health team at your side, guiding you and advising you which way to go. Your fellow recovery peers/friends are beside you cheering you on and practicing with you. Don't be afraid of taking risks! You are in the *best* place to practice and take risks in recovery! I remember my nutritionist saying to me when I was in treatment, "If you don't do it here, you won't do it outside of here." She said that to me as I was sitting at the dinner table debating on whether to eat dessert or not.

I did it; I ate my dessert, despite the feelings of guilt and shame that came along with doing so, my eating disorder screaming at me throughout every bite. I had to prove to myself that it *was okay* to eat foods that I had once not allowed myself to eat, food that I had labeled as "bad." To my surprise, I learned that I could enjoy those foods. And the world did not collapse because I had eaten dessert. My weight did not change. The food was actually delicious. I remember thinking to myself at that moment, *Wow, I've really been missing out.* Once leaving treatment, I didn't think twice about eating dessert when I felt like it, because I *knew* (I had proven it to myself in treatment) that I could have it—and enjoy it.

No one that hates food loves life.

When faced with challenges, feel the fear and do it anyway. Trust me; you will be glad you did once you are faced with a similar situation outside of treatment.

Treatment was the best decision I could have made when I knew I needed it.

**After moving back home for a while, I no longer had the option/opportunity to go to residential treatment. Residential treatment is expensive—by no means was I always going to be able to have that option would I relapse again. I did relapse several times and didn't have residential treatment to turn to.

I was able to meet with a therapist at some point, but she didn't have much experience with eating disorders, and I didn't feel like I was getting what I needed out of the sessions. There were no support groups in my area, not even in the state I was in. (I was recommended AA meetings at one point; it was the closest thing they had.) Feeling desperate, isolated, and alone, I sat down one day and thought about my options. As I searched the Internet for options, I came across the quote, *"Do what you can, where you are, with what you have."*

So what did I do?

I used my resources. I reached out for support to my friends in recovery, joined a few online support groups, and looked up motivational/recovery inspiration websites. I actually became stronger because I had no option other than to put the skills I had learned in treatment into real-world practice.

For a long time, I thought that I *couldn't* recover/do well without having the the support of the treatment center. I realized that I could. They had given me everything I needed to succeed. Now I needed to apply those skills. So with my "crutch" no longer in hand, I took a brave step forward, and even though I didn't know it at the time, I already carried with me everything that I needed to recover.

Hospitalization—Is it what you need?

When your eating disorder is so strong, hospitalization may be the best way to go. Once you get stabilized medically, you can be in a much better mind-set to fight your eating disorder. The sicker you are, the more irrational your thinking becomes. With stabilization, you are mentally and physically much stronger and actually able to work through the underlying emotional issues in therapy. *(Remember: it's not about the food—eating disorders are about so much more than that).*

"From a psychiatric perspective, hospitalization, in my opinion, is necessary when a patient experiences suicidal ideation, is borderline, and does not follow medication indications," states Dr. Kuthy.

"It is important to highlight that medical treatment, although crucial, is cut short if it is not accompanied by therapy and the help of a dietician. As highlighted before, eating disorder treatment is multidisciplinary—therapy, medical assistance, and dietary assistance are all key," adds Kuthy.

Dr. Hatchett agrees. "I cannot emphasize enough the importance of an integrated treatment approach. Medical treatment on its own will not provide any results."

As I gained health, I was able to see things differently. I felt better. Things were not so blurry and distorted and cloudy. I remember being able to *think and concentrate* again. With stability, you will see things differently. An eating disorder makes you see everything different, since you are seeing the world through an illness's eyes rather than your own. Keep choosing recovery and see for yourself how much clearer your vision gets.

8

The Recovery Process (One Day at a Time)

"Recovery is like doing the dishes . . . one plate at a time."
—Sarah, my sister in recovery

Recovery is a process, not an event.
Recovery is a process, not an event.
Recovery is a process, not an event.

It took a long time for that sentence to actually ring true for me. I had no idea what recovery was all about when I first began treatment. When I checked in to residential treatment for the first time in October of 2009, I thought that as soon as I walked out of there a few weeks later, I would be recovered completely.

Through my experience, I learned that recovery really is a *process*—not an event. I did not understand this until I walked the path myself. My friends in the recovery and treatment team would say this to me, but I didn't believe them. Only through experience, by walking the walk of recovery, did I begin to understand my own process. You learn as you go. And it is okay to be scared, to have doubts, to fear change. It is okay to feel all of this, as long as you keep moving forward by making healthy recovery choices—one day, one meal, or one moment at a time.

Many times, I felt like I was crawling instead of walking down the recovery lane. Many more times, I felt like I was moving backward instead of forward. I fell down *many* times. I stumbled, fell flat on my face, and didn't feel like standing up again. I didn't think I would be able to go on many times.

Recovery was not as simple and straightforward as it seemed. Robert Frost's quote "the only way out is through" were words I held on to (especially during the hard days) to help push through. However long I decided to stay on the ground when I fell—well, that varied. Sometimes I would stand up immediately, keep fighting, only to get immediately knocked down again. Other times I would be on my feet for a while, too scared to move forward, and turn back down the all-too-familiar yet deceiving and deadly path of anorexia. Other times, I walked—even danced—forward with confidence, and still got knocked down a lot of times. And that was perfectly okay.

At the end of the day, no matter how long I had been struggling, I could always choose to get back on the recovery track. *You can choose recovery at any given moment.* With practice and experience, I began to feel *good* the more I chose recovery. I felt better and better each time, more comfortable engaging in healthy—*fun* things—and *not ED behaviors*. It didn't feel good to be lying on the ground with my face in the dirt. It felt good to move away from what was causing me so much suffering, from what was trying to kill me. I began to feel empowered the more I chose recovery. Eventually, making recovery choices became the "norm" in my life and struggling with eating disorder behaviors was the strange thing. The gaps of recovery in my life and ED slips became further and further apart. Before I knew it, I didn't experience any more ED slips. Thoughts were present for a while, and eventually faded as I gave no importance to them. I no longer "fueled the fire" of those since I no longer engaged in behaviors or believed the thoughts which strengthened them. They became dim, dull, powerless little thoughts—fleeting—almost like a distant memory that is hard to recall in the back of my mind from time to time. And then—gone completely.

As you move forward in recovery, you will develop the capacity and confidence to overcome obstacles that you previously looked at fearfully. My perspective on what I could/couldn't do/achieve changed drastically throughout recovery. I would never take any of it back. I love the person who I am today, and a lot of how I am today I am because of the world I was able to do in my recovery from my eating disorder.

A note to my eating disorder

Dear ED: I am who I am not in spite of you, but because of you. I do not regret having had an eating disorder. You have been my most painful, yet greatest teacher. You have been my greatest source of growth, by forcing me to embark on an incredible journey of self-healing and awareness.

Stop comparing

My process of recovery was different from that of other people's. I finally stopped comparing myself to my friends I had met in treatment. We all had our own pace and journey of recovery to go through. Some people recover faster than others. I was able to make the most improvements in recovery when I stopped comparing myself to others and focused on taking care of *me*. (Taking care of myself instead of focusing on others was not something I was used to; this took a lot of practice).

Remind yourself that recovery really is a *process*. And your process is yours and yours only.

One day at a time

One of the things that helped me most throughout my journey of healing was to take recovery *one day at a time*. My mantra became *just today*. Taking recovery just one day, one meal, or one moment at a time reduced my anxiety *greatly*. Recovery became much more manageable. It was much less threatening and overwhelming for me to be present and deal with the moment at hand. Getting ahead of myself by stressing about things that hadn't even happened or might not ever happen overwhelmed me. Focus on *just today*. On just *right now*.

Eating "normally" again

I can still recall my first meal in residential treatment. I cried before the meal. I cried during the meal, and I cried after the meal.

And then I cried some more.

In that moment, I couldn't see what an accomplishment that first meal would be for me, how it marked a brave milestone in my journey of healing. It was the first of many accomplishments, which, summed together, would equal a full recovery from my eating disorder.

I believe I called my mom crying before the meal and told her in amazement what "they were making me eat." I told her I didn't want to eat that; that in no way was I ready to eat that meal my first night there. A million thoughts and emotions swarmed through me like a beehive inside of my brain. It was too much. *I can't do this. No. No.* A million thoughts and emotions swarmed through me like bees in a beehive. I can't do this. No. There is no way. My brain was so saturated with thoughts that all I can recall looking back is the feeling of unsurmountable anxiety. My heart was pounding loudly against my chest and tears were rolling down my face.

It doesn't matter what was going on inside my head at that moment. It would have been illogical of me to have expected to walk into treatment, instantly feel great, and have a smile on my face, enjoy all the food, and feel happy.

I felt miserable, sick, and scared. Everything scared me. People scared me, food scared me, life scared me. All of that was to be expected. I had a long way to go before I would feel good, much less even be convinced that I wanted to let go of my eating disorder in the first place.

What marked such an important step forward in my fight against my eating disorder as I ate my dinner that night was that I began to *participate in my recovery.* I ate my entire meal. *I acted against my eating disorder. Despite how miserable I felt, I did what I needed to do.* I wasn't just thinking about recovery or hoping to recover or imagining what life would be if I recovered. I was actually *doing* the work. This is choosing recovery.

Although I definitely believe in *mindful* eating and began to practice it in later recovery, I realize that for me, this wasn't possible in the early stages of my recovery. Sometimes I just needed to "do what I needed to do," to go through the motions of recovery. If my anxiety was in the roof and I had to eat a meal that greatly increased my anxiety, then I couldn't be mindful; instead, I would enjoy my food, eat slowly, and savor every bite. In fact, taking extra time and noticing the details/tastes in every food then probably would have caused my anxiety to only increase further. For a while, I didn't taste the food I ate. I ate mechanically and finished every bite *because I knew it was what I needed to do.* I chose recovery *again and again, and again and again—one day at a time,* because I knew that it was what I needed to do to recover. I didn't like it (okay, I hated it), I didn't feel like doing it, *but I did it anyway.*

No excuses. I chose the next best thing for my recovery again and again (one day, one meal, or one moment at a time), no matter what. I didn't give myself the option of **not** choosing recovery. I was going to recover, and I was going to make the choices I needed to make to recover.

"Wisdom means to choose now what will make sense later. I am learning every day to allow the space between where I am and where I want to be, to inspire me and not terrify me."
—Tracee Eliis Ross

Making healthy choices—choosing recovery over and over again *despite* what I was feeling or what was going on in my life, was something I would need to do—from that moment on—in order to beat anorexia.

Eating a balanced and regular meal plan—the first stages of

recovery—was, for lack of better words—painful, daunting and stressful. It seemed impossible for me to do it, let alone ever enjoy it again. I thought I would never get there. But I did. With time and persistence, eating became easier. It got easier each time I chose recovery because I began to get stronger, and I began to feel better. *I began to feed myself and fight against my eating disorder, instead of fight myself and feed my eating disorder.* I eventually reached a place where I not only ate without guilt, fear, anxiety, etc., but actually *loved* the food and the enjoyment of eating.

For a long time, I wanted to recover in all aspects **except** for one thing. obsessively wanted to hold on to an "ideal" weight number I had irrationally constructed in my head as being ideal for me. I wanted to recover my self-esteem, my joy for life, stabilize my mood, anxiety, depression and continue to maintain a certain weight. I didn't want to gain weight, not more than the weight I had decided that I would be comfortable at. As I got closer to the target range the team I worked with had decided was best for me, I approached the director of the treatment center. I told her that I would like to discuss my weight range goal with her (often referred to as Ideal Weight Range or IWR in treatment). I spoke to her as if I was proposing a business deal to a potential client. I said I was willing to settle at "x" weight, one I could compromise to that was neither what they recommended nor where I was currently at. We would meet in the middle. She said no; and I stormed away like a child, not understanding why she and everyone else were being so misunderstanding. I told her that I would like to discuss my IDW (ideal target weight range), that I would rather settle at "x" weight, one in which I would feel more comfortable. It was as if I was proposing a business deal to her to "settle" on a certain number. She said no; and I stormed away angrily, not understanding why she and everyone else were being so "misunderstanding."

Once leaving treatment, I fixated on my unhealthy "ideal" weight once again. I believed that by losing a few "extra" pounds (the difference between where I had wanted to be and where my treatment team recommended that I be) I would be comfortable and happy in my recovery. So I went through with that, convinced I was simply "settling where I was more comfortable."

I relapsed terribly.

Before I knew it, I was back at the treatment center. My anxiety didn't go away; it actually got much worse. I lost control and became overpowered by my eating disorder (it is always a trap to feel like "you are in control" when you are active in your eating disorder).

The first weeks of treatment and many times after, continued to hold on to this number. I thought that if I worked 100 in all other areas, then maybe, just maybe, I could recover without give up that seemingly minor detail.

After several incidents of relapse, falling on my face again and again and again and again— I finally understood (the hard way) that this was something that was simply impossible.

Simply put, you can't hold on to certain parts of your illness and recover at the same time. You either recover or you don't. I wish I had known this before having to relapse the many times that I did before doing so, which is why I am sharing this information with you. Don't waste your time or any more of your life by refusing to let go of every part of your eating disorder. Accept every part of recovery. Whatever feelings come up with doing so is exactly what you work through in therapy.

Feeling full

Once on a regular eating plan, I felt uncomfortably full throughout the day. This lasted for several weeks. The feeling of fullness made it that much harder to eat. My hunger signals were completely out of whack. I learned that this was normal. Since I had struggled with food behaviors for so long, my hunger signals were completely off balance. This would take some time. My hunger cues WOULD come back, with time. I needed to give my body time to readjust to a pattern of regular eating times again.

*I didn't realize how much food my body needed *just to be able to function.*

The meal plan I was given in treatment was the amount of food my body needed just to be able to function. If I were laying in a hospital bed all day, that is what I would need to eat to keep my organs and vitals functioning normally. I mentioned in an earlier chapter that I was assigned supplements to drink between meals. When I asked her about the supplements, she said to me what Nicole had mentioned previously, "The supplements are food for your brain, Vanessa. When your brain is malnourished, there is no way you can think properly." With that knowledge in mind, I began to look at food differently. I also began to feel the difference as my concentration improved, my ability to retain information came back, and my mood began to regulate. For moments, I began to actually *feel good*, to feel like myself again. As these periods of well-being increased and I began to feel better in more and more ways, my perception changed. I started looking at food as my *ally* instead of my enemy. Food was medicine. It fueled me not only physically but mentally and emotionally as well.

Food had never been the enemy after all; it never would be. My eating disorder was and would always be the enemy.

A Different Perspective

In today's fat-phobic society, it isn't uncommon to hear comments such as "Oh my God, this food that I am about to eat will go straight to x part of my body." If I could list all of the "fat comments" I hear in society right now I would need hundreds of pages to this book to go through them all.

I discussed what my nutritionist had said to me in that session with my mother, about how my views began to shift by looking at food as medicine for my recovery. She came up with a wonderful, different perspective. She offered this suggestion. Instead of looking at food and thinking, *Well, this is going to go straight to my (insert body part here)*, think of something like this: *This is going straight to my brain*. Or, *this food is going to keep my heart healthy*. Or, *this food is going to strengthen my bone density, preventing osteoporosis*. Or, how about, *This food is going to make my hair shiny and healthy, my skin clear, and bring color back to my face. This food is going to help me concentrate and be able to engage in things I love once again.*

I found this strategy to be so helpful. And it is true. It just depends on what you want to focus on. *Can you see all of the wonderful things food does for you?* If you can't think or feel that for yourself yet, just think about how miserable you feel by *not* having a healthy relationship with food. *Can you think of all the harm that that is doing to your body?* Food is not the enemy. Fat is not the enemy. An unhealthy relationship with food and fat phobias are the enemies.

I cannot say that eating wasn't difficult. It was. It was very mechanical at first. Especially those first weeks in treatment, many times my way to cope through a meal was to "just go through the motions," to just not think about it and do what I needed to do. (Sometimes this was the only way I managed to do it.)

Like I said, eventually eating became easier, manageable, and eventually enjoyable. The fullness went away, as did the intense binge cravings, and my hunger signals came back. Today, food is one of the things I love and enjoy the most about life. I can't imagine ever depriving myself of something so delicious again.

It's like the good wolf and the bad wolf. You get to choose which one to feed, and that is the one who will continue to grow stronger and stronger.

I had to choose to feed myself (and starve my ED) or feed my eating disorder (and starve myself). In recovery, I began feeding myself. I wasn't perfect; I would slip back more than once along the way, but each time I chose to feed myself instead of my eating disorder, I grew stronger against my illness. Eventually, I was strong enough to overpower my eating disorder. It had no use; it no longer served a purpose—covered a need in my life. I didn't need it. I never did, but I was finally healthy enough to realize that and had enough coping skills I could turn to instead of my eating disorder. Coping skills that actually *did* serve their purpose, that *accorded* with their name and made sense as part of living a healthy and full life.

Bite by bite, life started to get so much better. My appetite for food—and life—came back.

Every time you say NO to your eating disorder, you say YES to life. Focus on choosing recovery one day, one meal, or one moment at a time. Instead of stressing about what you are going to eat later on in the day, what you have already eaten, or "how much left" you have to go in recovery (because no one can tell you when you will reach a certain state of recovery; remember, this is a process and unique to each person), focus on what you need to do right now to get you closer to where you want to be.

Ask yourself: What do I need to do *right now* to get me closer to where I want to be? What do I need to do *in this moment* to recover?

Don't delay recovery.

"A year from now, you will wish you had started today."
—Karen Lamb

9 | Eating Mindfully

Practicing mindfulness throughout my day, especially during meals (mindful eating), was and continues to be a great tool for my emotional and mental health and well-being. *Mindful eating*—By being *present* during my meal, I was able to pace myself, to taste the food I was eating, and eventually, savor all of its flavors. I integrated all of my senses—smell, taste, touch, sound, and sight, to the event of eating. As I practiced eating with awareness, I felt at peace. I felt content and satisfied, not only with the food that was nourishing my body, but at ease in my body, and in my environment. I was able to actually enjoy the event, the presence of my surroundings, the person or people who were in my company. I was engaged. I felt whole. Completely present, I was able to savor not only the food, but the moment.

I was also much better able to cue into my body's hunger signals (since these were all messed up when I began recovery) and trust myself. After practicing mindful eating, listening and trusting my body, I moved on to intuitive eating, which I will discuss later in this chapter.

Affirmation for meals:

I will feed myself and fight my eating disorder, not fight myself and feed my eating disorder.

"There is more to eating than calories, even biochemically—there are vitamins, minerals, essential fatty acids, essential amino acids, antioxidants, electrolytes, fluids, dietary fiber, all the raw materials for repairing and remodeling every single cell in your body. More than that, there is culture, family history, occasion, artistry, skill, growth, feelings of joy or resentment, pleasure or distaste. There are emotional associations and memories, and there is the basic affirmation of life—'I need to eat to survive, and I am worth the effort to survive.' Every act of eating reaffirms your right to exist.

"There is more to movement than calories, even biochemically—there is bone strengthening, muscle building, aerobic fitness, neural growth, balancing of hormones and lipid transporters, and every single involuntary movement and chemical reaction carried on below your conscious awareness, working around the clock to stave off entropy. More than that, there is fun, adventure, challenge, mastery, strength, place associations, social bonding, the experience of being an alive thing on a round, blue speck in the galaxy. There is a basic affirmation that you exist in a world you were designed to navigate.

"Even if you are disabled, even if you have some impairment, your body is still exploring—from the bat of an eyelash to a trip to the bathroom. You are negotiating, discovering, and navigating a physical existence. You were made for this world. You belong in it, and it belongs to you. Eating and moving: your right to exist, and a world in which to exist. They are not rivals. They do not annihilate each other. They collaborate to make a whole person, body and soul."

—"Food and exercise are not matter and anti-matter," Michelle, blog writer of *The Fat Nutritionist*

10 | Things to Keep in Mind

"You can do more than just survive in this world; you can live in it. If you are willing to work hard on your recovery, you can transform your life into one that feels rewarding and fulfilling. This requires being patient, present, and accepting during all stages of your progress. It also means looking at yourself objectively, and getting to know who you really are. Choosing life means believing that someday—regardless of how long it takes—you will be free."
—Hall and Monika Ostroff, Anorexia Nervosa: A Guide to Recovery

Fault vs. responsibility

There's a difference between something being your *fault* and something being your *responsibility.* I carried a lot of shame when I was sick, and for a long time throughout my recovery. I felt ashamed and at fault for having an eating disorder.

It is not your *fault* that you developed an eating disorder, but it is your *responsibility* to choose recovery. Again and again and again. A quote by Josie Tuttle phrases this wonderfully: "It's not your fault that you developed an eating disorder or depression or an addiction or whatever else is trying to steal your life away. But it is your responsibility to save yourself. And you can."

Eating disorders are real illnesses. Like any illness, people struggling require professional treatment and support in order to recover. This doesn't take away the fact that you have the option of choosing recovery. While people can guide you and support you along the way, *you* have to be the one who is proactive and chooses recovery. You can make healthy decisions or you can choose to engage in unhealthy behaviors. *You have the choice to recover.* I am by no means saying that it is easy. It might be the hardest thing you will do. But you *can* do it. Only you decide whether or not to do what it takes to recover—whatever that entails.

You have to be serious about getting better. And doing so means choosing recovery no matter what. I had to choose recovery despite how I was feeling or whatever was going on in my life—again and again and again (and again, and again . . .).

There is no straightforward, easy answer or solution. There is no magic pill. I felt miserable, frustrated, and hopeless, many times throughout this. And I still had to choose recovery. *It won't always feel so bad. Things get better—so much better! On the other side of recovery there is LIFE, and it is there waiting for you to be a part of it. Just keep choosing recovery.*

Looking back today, I realize that fighting through (choosing recovery) the hard days was what ultimately strengthened me the most. If I was able to make it through the hard days choosing recovery, then it made it that much easier for me to choose recovery on the days that I felt much better. Don't give yourself the option of not choosing recovery.

> *"You cannot get much done in life*
> *if you only work on the days you feel good."*
> —Jerry West

You cannot pick and choose

When you decide that you want recovery (note: you may need to make this decision over and over again throughout your journey), you have to accept *everything* that comes along with recovery.

You cannot "kind of" hold on to your eating disorder and live your life at the same time. You cannot "pick and choose" in recovery, doing the things that feel "comfortable" in recovery and leaving out some parts of recovery that you would rather not deal with. You cannot live your life with one foot in an eating disorder, not even a toe or a fingernail. You can either choose to live, or choose to remain ill. Either you choose recovery, or you choose your eating disorder.

No matter where you are at in recovery right now, remember that you can choose **right now:** *Life or ED?*

If you are struggling, be honest and reach out to your support team. *Choose to make the best decision for your recovery right now.*

Note: Don't ever think that you are not "sick enough," "thin enough," or "worthy enough" to get help. Eating disorders are serious illnesses and everyone needs help to overcome them. If you are struggling, you deserve to get help. You don't have to do this alone.

Take action. Participate in your recovery.

Do what you need to do **right now** to stay in recovery.

You cannot move forward in recovery if you are malnourished.

I learned that eating well (following a balanced meal plan assigned to me by my dietician) helped stabilize my mood. This made the work I did in recovery *much easier.* Not only was my brain and body nourished, but food helped the medications I took work much better. I felt so much better. I could think clearly and actually see things—work things on from a much more rational mind-set.

"We can't solve problems by using the same kind of thinking we used when we created them."
—Albert Einstein

"Taking medications and not eating properly will *not* make you feel better," my treatment team would emphasize over and over again. "Medication can help, but FOOD is your medicine."

As hard as it may seem to do *what is right* despite *how you feel,* in recovery, you need to choose recovery above all else. My former therapist Natalie Frost said to me when I began recovery: *"It is your responsibility to feed yourself no matter what circumstances you're in."*

I could cry, scream, and complain all I wanted, but in the end, if I wanted to move forward, if I wanted to recover, **I had to choose recovery over my eating disorder, despite whatever was going on in my life.**

"This too shall pass." Riding the waves of recovery

Recovery has many ups and downs. Sometimes, recovery can seem relatively smooth and "easy," and other times, it can feel like a crazy roller coaster. When you feel like you are on that roller coaster and having a hard time, remember that *it will pass.*

Do your best to focus on *just today*. Take things just one day, one meal, or even one moment at a time. Being extra kind to yourself and enlisting extra support is always a great idea—especially when you are having a hard time.

Repeating positive affirmations to yourself, such as *"This too shall pass,"* or *"I have the strength and ability to make it through this, and I will,"* can be very helpful. It is important to keep in mind that **no feeling is permanent**. Things will get better as long you make the choices which bring you closer to health and happiness.

A friend of mine mentioned in group therapy once how the word *emotion* has the word *motion* in it. Motion, meaning that it is in movement, served as a reminder to me that any emotions I was experiencing would pass.

Don't be afraid of what you may feel as you choose recovery.

Just keep choosing recovery.

Feeling feelings

I had a difficult time identifying, feeling, and expressing my feelings as I let go of my eating disorder. When I was sick, I used my eating disorder to mask whatever uncomfortable emotions I was experiencing—fear, anxiety, anger, sadness, frustration, etc. I avoided my feelings and basic needs altogether when I was sick. So, naturally, as I let go of my eating disorder, I had to practice *feeling* my feelings. Sitting with my feelings, identifying them, and expressing them in the appropriate manner.

I didn't do this overnight. I was overwhelmed by everything I felt all at once. It's as if I had opened Pandora's Box and all of the emotions I had locked up for years spilled out of the box all at once. I felt I was swimming inside of the box, unsure of how to cope with so many intense feeling all at once. I didn't like what I was feeling, I didn't know how to cope with my emotions. I felt like a vulnerable child. I began having anxiety attacks* and an overwhelming sense of "I can't deal with what I'm feeling." Slowly, with the help of therapy, I began practicing different ways of expressing my feelings. **I could no longer turn to eating disorders to avoid uncomfortable feelings. In order to recover, I *had to feel.***

To do so, first I needed to:

1. Sit with the feeling. Literally, sit down and *experience* the feeling. *Feel* what was going on inside of me.
2. *Identify* the feeling. What is it that I'm feeling? (Sadness, anger, frustration, guilt, hopelessness, anxiety?) Put a name to the emotion.

If I was in a place where I felt safe enough to do so, I tried to identify what triggered the feeling(s). (If not, I went straight to Step 4, and came back to Step 3 when I felt ready to do so.)

3. Identify the cause—*what triggered or what is triggering this/ these feeling(s)?*

4. Ask myself—*what do I need right now?* What can I do **right now** to feel better?[2]*

Other times, I preferred painting or drawing. Writing has always been one of my favorite tools because by writing things down on paper, I no longer attempt to sort through all of the thoughts in my head as I have them fixed on paper. In this way, I often get a much clearer understanding of things. Even writing or doodling words that come into my would eventually help me get to the root of what was distressing me.

There are many ways to express yourself. If writing or art are not something you particularly enjoy, talking to a friend, dancing, singing or photography are only a few of the many coping skills out there which you can use. For more ideas, see *"Coping Skills"* at the end of this book.

Once you identify what you are feeling, then you can focus on dealing what triggers that feeling in a healthy way. This is where coping skills come into play again. It is important to learn new, healthy ways of working through emotions. Once you successfully identify your feelings and what it is that is triggering those feelings, you can address each of those triggers in a healthy way, one by one.

Let me give you an example of how I identified feelings and triggers when experiencing eating disorder urges:

Identify the feeling:

    Loneliness

2 "When experiencing this high degree of anxiety, the temporary use of an anti-anxiety medication helped me during panic attacks and to better manage what I was working on in therapy. As I learned to regulate these emotions on my own, my anxiety decreased and I relied less on the medication. If you feel like anxiety is preventing you from moving forward in recovery, interfering with your functioning and you find that you are not able to manage it on your own, you may want to consider discussing this with your team. Medications, in my opinion, can be a great tool to use as part of stabilization and wellness if used properly and only when absolutely necessary.

I am not a doctor or providing medical advice. Always consult your treatment team before making any recovery decisions such as the use of medications.

Identify the trigger(s): What is causing me to feel lonely?

I am feeling lonely because my friends canceled the plans that I had made with them to hang out.

What can I do to cope healthily?

Instead of restricting, I choose to call another friend to hang out with. If he/she is busy, I can always make plans with someone else or talk to someone on the phone.

This is an example put in the simplest terms, but it is a great way to begin practicing identifying feelings and triggers; a tool that is essential in eating disorder recovery.

Does recovery get easier?

I had a friend ask me once, "When does this get easier? I feel like the harder I work, the harder recovery gets." Sometimes, your eating disorder will fight you the further along you move forward in recovery. It's like your eating disorders final attempts to convince you to go back to it. (Comparing it to an abusive boyfriend, for example.) Recovery is a process of ups and downs. There are easier times and there will be harder times. The trick is to keep moving forward in recovery no matter what. It's kind of a two steps forward, one step back . . . four steps forward, one step back . . . seven steps forward, two steps backward kind of thing. In the end, though, you will have taken many more steps forward. You will look back one day and see *just how far you have come*. Be patient; this is a process (I cannot emphasize that word enough). One day at a time. And when the ED voices are especially loud in your ear, reach out and enlist extra support.

Optimist:
Someone who figures that taking a step backward after taking a step forward is not a disaster, it's a cha-cha.
—Robert Brault

Overwhelmed?

When things feel overwhelming, remember to:
- Breathe.
- Focus on one day, one meal, or one moment at a time. Focus on what you need to do *right now. Just today.*

Guilt for doing the right thing

As I practiced choosing recovery, I experienced a lot of *guilt* that came along with making healthy choices. Guilt for eating everything on my meal plan, guilt for not exercising, guilt for gaining weight, and so forth. If you are experiencing a lot of guilt while making recovery choices, know that this is not uncommon.

Jenni Schaefer discusses two different types of guilt in her book *Life Without Ed*: "Positive guilt is the kind of guilt you feel when you are doing the RIGHT thing. It's the kind of guilt your eating disorder makes you feel when you follow your meal plan. The kind of guilt you feel when you take a nap or spend the day at home relaxing because you are tired. The kind of guilt you feel when you TAKE CARE OF yourself, and not listen your eating disorder" (Schaefer, 2013).

I learned that *guilt* was another one of my eating disorder's tools to try to keep me trapped in it. *The guilt of being healthy and having needs is your eating disorder's way of attempting to pull you back to it*—to what "you deserve" to what is seemingly "comfortable," what "feels good" or "safe."

If you experience guilt **when you are making healthy choices,** remember that that is your eating disorder trying to lure you back into its deadly arms. Continue choosing recovery, despite feeling guilt or any other uncomfortable emotions, and cope with those feelings in a healthy way. You will not always have those feelings. *(eMotions!)* Eventually, making healthy choices will not only be a habit, but it will be pleasurable—enjoyable, and you won't have to think twice about it.

Guilt for doing the right thing means you're doing well; it means you're stepping out of your comfort zone. You are constantly faced with two important choices when recovering from an eating disorder: Either you act based upon how bad you feel and make unhealthy choices that will keep you trapped in your eating disorder, or you do what you need to do, and deal with the uncomfortable feelings that come up by coping healthily; as I have stated several times. The first choice means choosing illness, and the second choice means choosing recovery—choosing life. This is what recovery entails.Once again, it is normal to feel guilt during recovery process. The important thing is to keep choosing recovery, one choice at a time. The guilt will eventually go away.

Remember, recovery = life; ED = death.

What do you choose?

How illogical the idea that I experience guilt for eating. If I do not eat, I cannot survive. So am I supposed to feel guilty for living?
—Journal Entry, 2007

Your eating disorder is NEVER a solution to anything

No matter what situation you find yourself in, your eating disorder will *never* be the solution to *anything*. I read something once that said, *"Eating disorders promise to give you everything you want. Instead, they take away everything you need."* Everything your eating disorder says to you is a lie. Your weight will never be low enough for your eating disorder. You will die before you are "thin enough" or "good enough" for the illness. A powerful and true statement that I have heard is that "the best anorexic is dead." This applies to all eating disorders.

Always say NO to your eating disorder. Do not make it an option in your life anymore.

When eating disorder thoughts and urges resurface

Eating disorder thoughts and urges tend to resurface when you are stressed, anxious, or facing an uncomfortable situation. In this way, *eating disorder urges can serve purpose to let you know that there is something going on that you need to attend to.* Think of them as an alarm going off—alerting you to stop for a moment and attend to a *need.*

If you are experiencing urges, you can go back to the "Feeling Feelings list " and apply the same thing:

1. Sit with the *urge.* Literally, sit down and *experience* what you are feeling. *Feel* the urge.
2. *Identify* the urge (i.e., "I am experiencing the urge to binge right now" or "I really feel like restricting at my next meal"), and finally
3. Identify the cause—*what could be triggering this/these urge(s)?*

What is going on in your life that could be causing these eating disorder urges to come up? Are you worried about something? Are you nervous, anxious, scared, or angry about a situation?

If you are experiencing a "crisis" where you feel like you are overwhelmed with urges and don't feel like you can "sit with" what is going on, refer immediately to your 911 card or list and keep yourself safe. **This is why it is crucial to have a 911 prevention plan in place so you can have access to it if you are feeling especially vulnerable to engaging in your eating disorder.**

Keep in mind that your eating disorder served as a *coping mechanism* for the time that you were sick. Be gentle with yourself as you take time to learn new ways of coping and become comfortable with experiencing (often uncomfortable) feelings and emotions. Don't expect eating disorder thoughts to go away quickly. They will be there for awhile. The key thing to remember here is that *you are not your eating disorder; you are not your eating disorder thoughts.*

It is okay to have eating disorder thoughts **as long as you do not act upon them.**

Practice observing your thoughts, sitting with feelings and identifying them, and coping in new, adaptive manners. In therapy and with application, you can address the thoughts you have regarding your eating disorder and underlying central beliefs that fuel them. That is where you begin more intense work on changing your thoughts and belief system.

Avoid the scale

I never found it helpful, useful, or beneficial in any way to weigh myself in recovery. When I began treatment I would do blind weigh-ins. To this day, I believe it was one of the most astute things a client can do until they are further along in recovery. I always knew that no matter what number showed up on the scale, my eating disorder would not be satisfied.

Why set yourself up? If it triggers you to weigh yourself, don't do it. If you feel unsure about it, I would avoid doing so (play it safe rather than risk triggering yourself). My advice would be to let your doctor, therapist, or nutritionist monitor your weight, and discuss your feelings honestly with them. Together, you can come to an agreement about what is best for you. (It makes no sense to give a scale, a number, so much importance and significance in your life.) As I said, work with your team and be honest with them about your relationship with the scale.

Scales are for fish anyway.

I still don't weigh myself to this day. This isn't to say that I don't *know* approximately how much I weigh; the point is that I don't give any extra time or go out of my way to give an insignificant number any importance. The number on the scale, like any number, does not define me as a person.

Becoming comfortable knowing what your weight range is *versus* constantly weighing yourself or letting the number on the scale dictate how you are going to go about your day are two very different things. Leslie Laney Hale, my former dietician and current RD at Tapestry Treatment Center in Brevard, North Carolina, offers this important advice:

"I think that it is important for a patient to get to a place where they are comfortable knowing what their weight range is before leaving treatment. I think a relapse could arise when a patient leaves treatment and is surprised by their weight. An important step to recovery is finding peace with being at a healthy weight. If you do not accept your body's 'healthy weight,' you can not fully recover from an eating disorder—in my opinion."

"Scales only have the power which we bestow upon them. In reality, a scale is just a small household item made of metal & springs & dials. A scale is a toaster is a blender is an electric toothbrush is a weed whacker. Imagine if I said, 'My self-worth is determined by the toaster.' Sounds pretty weird, eh? Or, 'I'm fat, the lawnmower said so!' Or, 'I have to check with the blender to see if I like myself today.' The power only comes in when we choose to hand all of ours over—to an inanimate object."
—Kensington, SomethingFishy.org

Labeling foods as "good" or "bad"

Labeling foods as "good" or "bad" is another one of ED's rules on his infinite list of irrational, abusive rules. As soon as I went into treatment, I learned to "take off *all* labels." Food is food. There are no "good" or "bad" foods. No food is good or bad for you. Just as much as you need to include vegetables in your meal plan, your body also requires nutrients from other foods like sweets, fats, carbohydrates, protein, etc. Different foods offer different nutrients that your brain and body *need* to be healthy. Different foods make up a healthy, balanced meal plan. Take off those labels. Balance is key here. And if you think of "dieting" as an option during or after recovery, throw that idea into the trash. The first three letters of diet spell out the danger. A healthy balanced nutrition plan includes *all* foods, *unless you struggle with diabetes, certain food allergies, etc.—which is why I suggest your meal plan always be provided to you by a RD, medical professional, or your treatment team.*

I stopped looking at calorie content. Something I would do in treatment was grab a Sharpie and cross out the nutritional content on the back of the packages. Calories are no more than units of heat energy. What's important is what the food does provide, the nutritional content which makes it up. I wasn't going to do this the rest of my life. It's not like I imagined myself years from then rushing home from the supermarket and Sharpie-ing all of the nutrition information on every food item in my house. No. But it *is* something that helped me in that moment. And so I did it.

Take the focus off of labels and numbers. Say good-bye to them.

Eating "100 percent healthy" is not healthy.

Keep in mind that "eating 100 percent healthy foods" is *not* healthy. My eating disorder started that way, and it was a struggle for me to let go of that throughout recovery. Remember, you *need all* foods.

A diet/meal plan that prohibits certain foods is *not healthy*. It is a big red flag of disordered eating in families and setting people up for eating disorders.

- Other reason: helps avoid bingeing.

Leslie Laney Hale agrees:

"In my opinion, ALL food is good food. When we put labels on food, we create a negative tone toward certain foods that is not helpful for anyone, especially if in recovery from an eating disorder. Whether it is a cookie or an apple, there are positive qualities about all foods. My personal belief is 'All Foods in Moderation,' and that is something I stress to my clients so they do not focus on 'good foods' and 'bad foods.'"

"Fat" days

Days when you are "feeling fat." If you have been in recovery for a while, you may have already heard that *fat* is not a feeling, but a lot of the times when you are feeling uncomfortable, you automatically turn to "fat" as a feeling. Sometimes it's tough to identify what you are *actually* feeling (i.e., anxious, frustrated, sad, etc.) when you are feeling so uncomfortable in your skin. When this happens, do your best to not focus on your body—avoid looking at mirrors, weighing yourself. Take the focus off of your body if you just can't seem to feel comfortable in your skin that day. Instead, do something nice for yourself—paint your nails, grab some coffee with a friend—anything to take your mind off of what is bothering you. I would collage my mirrors with positive quotes and images. Body sabotaging only contributes to low self-esteem and increasing distorted thoughts and urges.

Turn to your friends. Let them be your mirrors if you are having a hard time looking into one and hear what they have to say about you. You will be surprised. Observe a baby during bath time. Notice how a baby is cheerful, curious and playful in their skin. They are not sabotaging their body, pinching their cheeks or fat on their little thighs. Watch children playing outside. Notice how they use their body to play, jump, explore, experience and engage in life. *This is your nature.* Love and accept your body and all of who you are.

"Making up" for eating "extra"

I've heard this often from people struggling with eating disorders. Feeling the need to restrict or exercise more, to "make up" for eating "extra" one day, during the holidays or while on vacation. All of this is another eating disorder trap. Let it go. The only thing that such thinking will do (besides wasting valuable energy and time) is open the doors for eating disorder urges to come in at full force. This is another eating disorder trap. So as far as feeling like you need to "make up" for what you ate at any point, remember—*you don't.*

Making adjustments in the real world

I will touch on this topic further along in this book. Life is flexible, constantly changing. It is not structured like a treatment center or hospital. *Your meal plan is your guide.* As you move further along in recovery, you can begin "moving things around," alternating exchanges here and there, eating out and not stressing out about not following what is exactly "written" on your meal plan. This goes together with mindful eating and intuitive eating. In early recovery it is common and advisable to follow your meal plan exactly as it is. It gives you structure and normality as you adjust to eating properly. Later on, instead of following it like a bible you can use it as a guide, something you have in the back of your head. You will begin to let go of the rigidity of your meal plan as you learn to trust your body and know what you need to eat in order to be healthy.

Progress, not perfection

Aim for progress, not perfection. Perfection doesn't exist; it is some sort of grandiose idea that the society has constructed of a reality that doesn't even exist. What is "perfection" anyway? What defines "perfect body?" or a "perfect life?" I've never heard of either. Yet, here we find ourselves, chasing the idea of something irrational, and always falling short when we "are not perfect." Whether we are talking about eating disorder recovery, school, a job, goals, a relationship, a lifestyle, or anything; what is key to remember is that 1) perfection doesn't exist, 2) the only person you need to focus on being "better than" is your past self; or improving in an area that you want to feel better in in your life.

Aim for progress in your recovery. Be kind to yourself, applaud your successes and when you struggle, just make the next healthy choice for your recovery.

Advice for over-exercisers

I used to struggle with over-exercising. Eventually, my body began to give out. Your body can only push its limits for so long . . . We are not machines. We are human beings. The effects of over-exercising can be incredibly debilitating physically, mentally, and emotionally.

I got to the point where the pain of exercising as part of my eating disorder felt more exhausting mentally and emotionally than physically. It was as if someone was forcing me to abuse myself, to push my body to its limits, to keep going, to never stop. (In this case, my ED was, as it had for a long time, but it was no longer "working" as a coping skill for me.) Like everything with an eating disorder, the "temporary" feeling of satisfaction eventually wears away and all you can feel is the real torture that it is causing you. And by that point, you feel like you *can't stop*. Even if you want to. This is the addictive hook that plays part in eating disorders. I was abusing my body. I didn't stop over-exercising until I was forced to, after fracturing my foot due to exercising hours on end. I had no choice but to STOP and—rest. At first, I felt petrified, upset, and angry. (This was my ED voice screaming in my head.) But it was the biggest blessing I could have received. Finally, I felt like I could *breathe*. I could relax. I didn't "have to" exercise since I physically couldn't.

I had that time period to slow down in my life and realize/reflect on a lot of things. I started picking up other activities that I had left, started enjoying myself more and just enjoyed *being* rather than *doing*.

- Shortly after this incident, I received a bone density test to check the health of my bones. I was 18 years old and fell into the category of *osteoporosis*. The doctors there couldn't even give me an "official" diagnosis because of my age—most people who receive bone density exams are well over 18. This was one of my first eye-openers into the consequences that my illness was having on my body.

- Luckily, bone density at my age was *reversible*.

I was incredibly lucky.

I have friends who over-exercised compulsively to the point where they can no longer exercise because of permanent health conditions (caused by compulsive exercise, another aspect of their eating disorders, or both). I have a friend who used to love running, but after overdoing it for a long time, now she can only walk very slowly for a certain amount of time, monitored. I have friends who choose to no longer exercise since they recovered. Instead, they fill their day with activities to meet their physical health goals without having to go to the gym or even put on tennis shoes. Gardening, walking, doing things around the house. Choose to do that is *fun* for you. If exercising isn't *enjoyable* for you, if it's more of a mundane *chore* than a playful activity that is actually *fun*, it is doing you no good. Physically, mentally, and emotionally, it is debilitating and harmful.

Slow down. If exercise is part of your eating disorder, speak to your team *immediately*. Stop over-exercising—or exercising compulsively before it's too late. Stop doing something that you may regret in the long run. Pun intended.

Listen to your body . . . or eventually it will force you to.

Since beginning treatment for my eating disorder, I stopped exercising for a long time before slowly easing back into it over a year later. I followed the instructions that were given to me by my dietician. A limited amount of exercise, a limited amount of time each week. And if I didn't exercise at all, I didn't eat any less than I knew I needed if I exercised less or didn't at all. There were moments my meal plan was adjusted for days I did exercise—adding an extra snack following a workout. I planned this out carefully with my nutritionist, trusting (you need to do this in recovery) that she would know what was best for me (as she was trained in that). The amount of exercise that was prescribed to me as part of my recovery plan is the "maximum" that I would allow myself to do.

This can all seem very precise and detailed in recovery, and by all means, follow your recovery plan to a T for as long as you need to. That is what worked for me. Only then was I able to trust myself, my body, as I witnessed that what I was doing was working.

Today, I have a much more balanced and mindful approach towards exercise. If I choose to not exercise; I continue to eat what I need to eat. I don't eat any less than I would on a day I would exercise, I usually eat more. As you move further along in recovery, with practice, everything will become more and more natural—eating what you know you need to eat, exercising moderately, etc.

It's like riding a bicycle or learning something new for the first time. In the beginning your mind is filled with so many things—you are trying to think of everything you need to do and do a lot of things at once so as to not fall off the bicycle. With practice (and falling several times), muscle memory eventually kicks in. Before you know it you are enjoying the ride instead of focusing on not falling.

Recovery is the same.

Stick to the basics for as long as you eat. If you are ready to exercise, then do so according to what is healthy for you. Make sure you are enjoying yourself. If exercise isn't fun, if you are experiencing ED-fueled thoughts such as "I need to exercise for x amount of time," "I need to exercise more if I'm going to eat out later," if you feel miserable while exercising, if it feels like a chore, or if you experience guilt when you're not doing so—then do not engage in it as it is still a part of your eating disorder. Talk to your team about this.

Don't worry if you're not where you want to be yet, everything takes time. It is better to address every area that your eating disorder impacts and work through it step by step than continuing to engage in anything that fuels it. I've had people ask me things like "but *when* will I be able to exercise normally again?" or "I used to love dancing and I just want to enjoy it like I used to."

You will. Personally, I have a much healthier relationship with exercise (like food) today than I did before even having had an eating disorder. Whether it be running, playing tennis, swimming, or rock climbing, I make it a point to only exercise if I am enjoying myself. The moment I find that I'm not, I stop what I'm doing.

College sports

I received a full scholarship to play tennis at a D1 university. With my eating disorder at full force, playing competitive college tennis and loading up my semester with premedical courses, my schedule became more and more intense as the weeks went on. I would wake-up at 5 A.M. to train, went to class all day, trained in the afternoon, attended science labs after that, and with my eating disorder convincing me to that that was simply not enough—I would exercise some more. That, continued with nights of organic chemistry and anatomy homework until 2 A.M.—with limited food intake—took an expensive toll on me. I collapsed, physically, mentally, and emotionally. The only thing that kept me going at that point was my faith. I prayed to God. And I trusted my heart to tell me what was right. I listened to the inner voice inside of me (not my eating disorder, but *myself*), the one that was crying out for help and told me I needed to stop what I was doing.

I dropped out of the tennis team. The sport I loved and had played my entire life had become compulsive; it had become a mechanism of my eating disorder. Eating disorders take over *everything* in your life, sucking out the joy of *every single thing* you could ever enjoy. Eating disorders have no tolerance; they leave absolutely no room for happiness.

Later in recovery, I considered playing tennis again for college and at another point thought about trying out for the cross-country team. I thought about my options carefully. I wanted to dive right into them. I was feeling so great that I wanted to once again "take back" what my eating disorder had taken away from me. But I had to be careful. I could not rush back into things and immerse myself into potential triggers. Although I was doing much better, I had to (and still do) take a lot of things into consideration before doing them.

I came to the conclusion on both occasions that playing a competitive sport was *not* something I thought was a good idea. The healthier choice for me, for my recovery, was moderation when it came to exercising. The risk of relapsing into overexercising was too high, even if I had the intentions of competing "for fun." How did I come to this conclusion? There were several points I considered to rule against my recovery:

- Pressure: I knew that once competing, the pressure would be high. For me, at least, playing with some sort of pressure (to maintain a certain level, number of wins) took the enjoyment out of what I was doing. Pressure to train harder, more hours, could easily push me to a breaking point.
- Time: Being a student athlete really means dedicating almost all of your time to your sport and your remaining time to schoolwork .You go to school, and then you are at practice all afternoon. But it is not only that. When you are not at school or at practice, you are often in the training room, icing, stretching, or doing extra practice with your coach. On the weekends and on weekdays, you are traveling to away matches (or meets), which takes a full day up to a full week. This comes with a lot of stress, and it didn't offer me the balance that I really needed in order to succeed in recovery. I needed balance, and I needed *less* things on my to-do list . . . not more.
- No set routine: This is another big point. Forget structure. Missing class, eating on the road, doing homework in the car were norms of college sports. *Not that any of this isn't amazing. It is. But I couldn't have done that at that point, not unless I was fully recovered for a significant period of time—where I could have that flexibility and manage stress and changes without it affecting my health.* Once fully recovered, it still would be something I would think twice about before committing to it.

In that moment, I chose to *not* participate in any college sports, take a lighter course load, and focus on my recovery. I chose to engage in other activities which brought genuine joy to me and didn't risk my recovery. With this, I really want to emphasize the importance of identifying your triggers and keeping them in the back of your mind throughout your life. If you know what triggers you, it can prevent you from struggling and enable you to handle the situation differently.

Comparisons in treatment

Residential treatment is an interesting playground. You are in an environment where there is both wonderful people sharing the same goal as you—healing and recovering their life. Bonds made in these kinds of situations many times forge friendships that last a lifetime. At the same time, you are in an environment where everyone's eating disorders are—imprisoned, furious, powerless. These illnesses seem to have a mind of their own, and it can be a battle to be in treatment fighting for recovery while facing triggering situations left and right eating disorder behaviors being sneaked by, feeling the pull of your own illness when other eating disorder behaviors are present, wanting to give up when others feel that is the best option. At the same time—seeing others thriving and taking steps forward in their recovery—watching them transform (this is what I honestly see with people in recovery)—can bring about a mixture of feelings. Feeling proud and inspired and at the same time frustrated for feeling like you are not there yet.

Try to focus on you and only you. Everyone IS there to heal (although not everyone is ready for it); and at the same time everyone there is coming in with their eating disorder very present and strong. *Take care of you and protect your recovery.* (It's OK and healthy to say if something is triggering you.)

Your eating disorder will always try to compare you to others. Don't do it. You are you. And you are fabulous and beautiful because you are *you*. Bestselling author and speaker John Mason named one of his books: *You're Born an Original, Don't Die a Copy.*

Whether you are in an inpatient treatment setting, residential treatment center, or outside of a treatment, the same rules apply. *Triggers are everywhere.* Don't let them affect you. Choose to not be pulled or moved by them. Just don't. That is your eating disorder trying to grab any excuse to lure you back Remember you have a choice. *Focus on you. Take care of you.*

Tip: Surround yourself with people that love you and believe in you. People who are supportive in your recovery and believe in your dreams. Surround yourself with people who help you move forward in recovery and not pull you back into the illness or keep you stuck.

Stay close with friends in recovery who *want* recovery. It didn't matter if I was struggling or if my closest friends in recovery were struggling. The important thing was that, at the end of the day, we were all fighting for freedom. We actively chose recovery and did our best to support and motivate each other. Unfortunately, I met many individuals in recovery who gave up on treatment, chose their illnesses over recovery, or felt like they would never recover. I do believe everyone truly wants recovery (who would really want to suffer with something like that?), but as I said, not everyone is ready for it, believe they can recover, or become too sick to recover due to other health consequences.

Everyone can recover from an eating disorder, but eating disorders place your life on a ticking time bomb. The sooner you choose recovery, the better off you will be in every sense—mentally, emotionally and physically. Life without an eating disorder is not guaranteed anyway, so you deserve every single moment you have on this earth to be filled with just that—life and freedom.

Pro-Ana-Mia Websites

There is a tremendous about of websites, blogs, and other social networking --- that *promote* eating disorders. Website that *glamorize* emaciation, eating disorders as a lifestyle and glorify mental illness. The people who run these sites are *very ill*. Sadly, many going these groups, many of whom are very sick in their eating disorders or prone to falling ill.

There is nothing "glamorous" about eating disorders. Eating disorders have the highest mortality rate of any mental illness. These websites are toxic and dangerous. Although there are organizations that exist to take down Pro-Ana and Mia websites; with so much access to the Internet—one gets taken down and others are already getting put up.

It is important to be aware that these pages exist. Just as important, there will be triggers everywhere if you look for them. But they do not have to hurt you if make a proactive choice to avoid them. *Protect your recovery.*

Stay away from anything that is detrimental to your recovery. This may include fashion magazines, certain websites, social media applications, diet articles, etc. Put on your invisible shield and keep walking the bold, brave walk of recovery. Do not allow anything to contaminate your wellbeing.

On the other hand, there are many healthy and motivational resources online that you can turn to to stay motivated and supported in recovery. The benefit of online resources is that you can access them from any place and time as long as you have access to the internet.

Here are some options:
- Websites that promote recovery: pro-recovery websites, pro-recovery blogs from people who have recovered or are in recovery, articles written by eating disorder survivors.
- Pro-recovery support groups and forums. (www.something-fishy.org) is a popular and excellent website that provides information to people in recovery as well as family members and friends. The website includes support forums that are available 24/7 and moderated at all times to ensure that they promote health. This is a great way to reach out and receive support and inspiration from others who have recovered or are in recovery.
- This isn't the only online support group available online. There are plenty. Research your options and make sure to check the

validity of the website before joining. A benefit of these pages is that you can post anonymously and freely express what you are experiencing.

- Recovery inspiration videos, quotes and photos available at all times.

You need to take action.

"A real decision is measured by the fact that you've taken a new action. If there's no action, you haven't truly decided."
—Tony Robbins

I mentioned this briefly in the previous chapters. In order to recover from your eating disorder, you need to *participate* in your recovery. You need to take action. Therapy, medications, and having a solid support network by your side are essential and helpful, but in the end only you are the one who can let go of your eating disorder—by choosing recovery again and again.

Choosing recovery. No matter what.

There will be times when you fall flat on your face. Sometimes you will feel like you won't be able to get up. Or that, no matter how many times you get up, you keep falling. It's okay. Stand up and *keep going*. For those of us who have recovered, know that none of us would have gotten to where we are had we quit at one point.

I am not saying this is easy. Recovering from an eating disorder is the most difficult thing I have ever done in my life. But it has also been the most rewarding and worthwhile experience. I would not take it back for anything. I cannot put into words *all of the gifts* recovery has given me. All of the gifts. It has given me back my life. A life filled with joy, gratitude, health, peace, and inner freedom I never thought possible. I am sure that I would not be as thankful, at peace, or as present in my life had I never had an eating disorder to begin with. I am not saying I am thankful that I had an eating disorder, but

I do not regret having had it. I am incredibly thankful for recovery. It has given me what no other experience could have given me.

The emotional work of recovery involved taking the bandages off the emotional wounds I wasn't addressing. That is what an eating disorder does. It puts band aids over open wounds. You avoid them by coping with an eating disorder; pretending they don't exist because you cannot "see them," but they are there. Like an open wound in the flesh, an emotional wound only gets worse until you finally decide to treat it. In recovery, I took the band aids off. All of them. One by one made it more manageable. As difficult as it was, by addressing each underlying issue, I began to heal inside. And just like physical wounds, the emotional ones began to close.

"Until you heal the wounds of your past, you will continue to bleed. You can bandage the bleeding with food, with alcohol, with drugs, with work, with cigarettes, with sex, but eventually, it will all ooze through and stain your life. You must find the strength to open the wounds, stick your hands inside, pull out the core of the pain that is holding you in your past, the memories, and make peace with them."
—Iyanla Vanzant

Consequentially, I realized that my past fears were just that—my past, an illusion and not my present reality. I carried with me the lessons I learned through each experience. Any wound leaves a mark once it heals, one that can always remind you of the lesson learned throughout its healing. I acquired more insight as time went on, addressed emotionally what I was in the habit of ignoring, and focused on doing what I had to do to keep moving forward.

I wasn't perfect, I never will be. Accepting that was an important part of the work I did, I mentioned this earlier. Today, I choose to honor and accept who I am, where I am, and strive to move forward; to be a better person each day. I do my best, and that is enough; as it is all I can do. The idea of "not good enough," like the idea of perfection, is another illusion. You cannot do better than your best effort. Trying your hardest *is* your best at that particular moment in time. So let go of the end result and focus on what you are doing. Remember, the only way to fail in life, as author Johanna de Silento states wonderfully, is to abstain: "You have a whole lifetime, time takes time. The only way to fail at life is to abstain." Participate in life, don't abstain from it. Abstain from your eating disorder. Don't give up on life or on yourself.

> *"Failing is not falling down but staying down."*
> —Mary Pickford

Never give up. Keep choosing recovery (no matter what) and applaud yourself every single step of the way.

Get out of your HEAD!

When you can't seem to fight the negative thoughts in your head, sometimes the best thing to do is get out of your head. **Change the scene**. Get outside. Go to a bookstore. Call up a friend you can socialize with. Change your environment and distract yourself. Do fun things with friends you feel comfortable with and with whom you can be yourself. Surround yourself with healthy individuals. If the people you often reach out to are not healthy for you, then aim to reach out to those who are. Meet new people, establish new friendships. Take your mind off of your eating disorder. Take classes, work, volunteer, learn a new hobby, try something you've always wanted to do and haven't. Right now is the time to rediscover your interests—to rediscover yourself. Without your eating disorder in your life, you have room for the infinite things life has to offer. Try something new. Try a lot of things. Stay active (mentally) and surround yourself with positive things, positive people, and fill your time with things that fulfill you—that make you feel good inside.

Acting Opposite—Distress Tolerance

Everything your eating disorder "feeds you" is a LIE. Always act opposite to what your eating disorder tells you. This is known as distress tolerance.

I know it's difficult to do in the moment, but it gets easier. You will eventually feel better each time you chose to not listen to your eating disorder. The more you fight your eating disorder, the more healthy decisions you make, the weaker the illness gets. As you get stronger, your eating disorder will get weaker. But you need to get stronger for your eating disorder to get weaker, and the only way to do that is to choose recovery over and over and over again. It will become a habit and before you know it, you won't think twice about listening to your illness. It just isn't an option. You won't need to follow through with an eating disorder behavior because you will have acquired new, healthy coping skills that actually make you feel good and are good for you.

Live. You cannot live and enjoy your family and be YOU or laugh or really have a good time with friends or actively participate in life with an eating disorder. Ultimately, you need to choose. Life or eating disorder. Of these two options, only one has a future. You deserve a beautiful life. Choice by choice, choose recovery. You can do this.

Excuses in recovery

I mentioned previously that not exercising in no way meant I would restrict on food. The idea that not exercising = "can't eat/must restrict" is a *disordered* thought. Similarly, holding on to similar excuses (i.e. not exercising so I can eat less) will only prevent you from making a full recovery. You cannot put off recovery. You cannot recover when something changes, if something happens, or only under certain conditions.

I will recover when _____.

I will recover if _____.

I will recover only if _____.

Cancel these sentences out of your mind. This does not work. You either make excuses or you make progress. But you can't make both. We wouldn't make much progress if we only worked on the days we felt good. You can't put off recovery. If you wait for the "will to recover" or the "motivation to recover," or anything to initiate action in recovery, then you could literally be waiting around until you die.

You have to let go of excuses and exceptions. Again, I am not saying that recovery is easy. But it *is* possible, and it is definitely worth it. And the only way you are going to recover is if you **do recovery;** if you take action. You can think about, dream about, or wish for recovery all day long. In the end, though, you need to choose recovery for as long as you need to until you are fully recovered. Conditions will never be perfect for you to take care of yourself and begin living your life. The best time to choose recovery, to change your life for the better, is *right now.* Do not wait around in misery. Start choosing recovery and keep on choosing recovery right now.

"A year from now, you will wish you had started today."
–Karen Lamb

Looking at the harsh reality

It can be hard to find motivation when the going gets tough. Something that helped me move forward and make healthy choices when I really did not feel good or feel like recovering was **making a list of reasons as to what would happen if I decided to go back to my eating disorder, and putting it somewhere where I could see it every day.**

So, you feel like giving up? You want to throw in the towel and go back to your eating disorder? Having doubts if recovery is really for you? Is it really worth it? Will you just be "fat and miserable" after all of this?

The reality is:

Recovery = life. (A life worth living.)
ED = death. (Dead or alive.)
Living to live vs. living to die.

You have to think about the consequences. If you engage in an eating disorder behavior *right now*, what will happen? What's going to happen if you keep choosing your eating disorder over recovery down the line? Get sicker and sicker . . . go to a treatment center? Go to another treatment center? Feel miserable, watch everyone continue on with their life and watch everything slip away from you? Isolate yourself from the world, from your dreams, joy, everything except illness. End up in a hospital; psychiatric of medical—you choose, you will probably end up in both. Suffer from irreparable medical consequence while those you love cry at your side as they watch you fade away from life into a shell of the wonderful human being you are?

Die?

When I at my worst point with the illness, I believed I was in control of it. It was the exact opposite. I was NOT in control. I was losing more and more control over my life as I gave more power to my illness. I began to lose the freedom of my own decisions—the most vital aspect that gives a person their individuality, their identity. I was too clouded by the disorder at that point to see this. When I spoke with a therapist one day, convinced and relaying to her that I simply "could not eat," her response was something that struck a painful nerve in me:

"Well, if you cannot physically feed yourself, then other people are going to have to make decisions for your life. You will have to unwillingly go someplace where you can be fed."

I have no words to explain how humiliated, ashamed, and sick I felt in that moment. Her words stung me like hydrochloric acid on an open wound. *Go someplace where you can be fed… other people are going to have to make decisions for your life."*

What she said to rang with utter truth. I had nearly *zero* power over my decisions at that point. Would I continue to go down the eating disorder path, then I could say goodbye to my life, even while alive. My choices, my voice, my very own will.

There are things you hear in your life that struck you will a painful reality, that awaken you. Things that ignite strength inside of you, and compel you to grab hold of it with unwilling wit and make the changes—as difficult as they may seem or as far away from your goal as where you want to be—to make a change to better your life. Something that motivates you in a way that few things in your life do, something that you know you have to do to give yourself the life you deserve.

The words I heard in that moment were just that for me. A painful yet necessary reality that to this day I am grateful I heard. They were exactly what I needed to hear. The only person who would ultimately be in charge of my life, despite having the support of others around me—was me.

Sticking to recovery is hard, but you can choose to stay in recovery. It gets better, and even when it's really difficult and you feel like quitting, it's always better than living in the hell (a short-lived sense of accomplishment) of an ED. Kate Le Page, author of *Goodbye, Ana,* couldn't have said it better: "My worst days in recovery are better than my best days in relapse."

Choose *life*. Think about all the wonderful things life has to offer and how good you feel when you're HEALTHY and can think clearly, move, jump, play, laugh, and live. If you can't think of how great healthy feels, then look at where you *don't* want to be. Depressed? Sick? Fragile? Cold? Sad? Anxious? Alone? Scared? Isolated? Tormented by the same, miserable thoughts?

If you can't remember about a time in your life when you felt happy and "free" of your ED, then how about giving recovery a shot? You know what it's like to suffer with an eating disorder and "live" in that miserable hell. But do you know what life after recovery is all about?

You might as well give recovery a try. You have absolutely nothing to lose and everything to gain by doing so. I can't describe life after an eating disorder to before it—it is not even comparable or can be put into words.

Try it out for yourself and see. Live the answer.

"What if I told you 10 years from now your life would be exactly the same. Doubt you'd be happy. So why are you afraid of change?"
—*Karen Salmansohn*

11 | Stepping Out of Your Comfort Zone

It was a leap, not a fall.

"As someone trying to recover, you have to make the choice to take the leap or to stand on the precipice forever. Recovery can't be something you dip your toe into. For it to be fully felt and completely comprehended, you have to immerse yourself."
—Carolyn Costin, Founder and Executive Director of Monte Nido and Affiliates

Don't be afraid to step out of your comfort zone in recovery. If you *do not* feel uncomfortable in recovery, you probably aren't making much progress. Feeling uncomfortable shows that you are stepping out of your comfort zone, moving away from your perceived sense of "safety"—away from your eating disorder. You are moving forward in recovery, you are moving toward something that isn't so "seemingly" secure, but instead, open to a world of possibilities—life.

Be proud of yourself as you take steps forward. As you become more experienced, more confident with yourself, acquire new skills and refine them to cope with life in a healthy way and make your way through recovery, you will feel better and better. Remember—you won't always feel so uncomfortable, and feeling that way is part of making progress. Be patient with yourself. I will not get tired of repeating this: *recovery is a process*. Keep going.

Only look back to see how far you've come

If you keep choosing recovery, you will move further and further along much quicker than you can imagine. It's as if you are climbing a mountain. You climb and you climb and you climb, but you still haven't reached the top. You feel like you will never get there. When you look back, however, you realize just how far you've climbed. How small all the little details behind you are. And even if the top still seems far away, what was once in front of you is long behind you. And it isn't so scary anymore looking back. Things aren't as big and overwhelming as they seem when you look at them from as distance as opposed to seeing them head on. It is all about perspective. Recovery will give you a new perspective on life. You can't see the world clearly with an eating disorder—an eating disorder distorts reality. Remember it leaves no room for anything other than itself; as you cannot see or experience anything beyond it.

Embracing your healthy and natural body

Before I could love my body at its natural weight, I had to accept it. In order to accept my body at whatever weight it was meant to be at, I was going to have to feel uncomfortable (yep, it's just part of it) for some time as I got used to how I felt in my body being healthy. Accept, accept, accept. Do your best to not resist these necessary changes. You won't always feel this way, and it's something you need to do to get you to full recovery.

As my weight increased, my physical body became healthier, and my body began to function normally again. Although I felt like crawling out of my skin every waking hour, I began to experience what being healthy felt like. Mentally as well. My hair grew thicker and shiny again, my skin was no longer flaky and dry, my nails hardened and no longer broke, the purple circles under my eyes faded away, color came back into my cheeks, and my eyes lit up with—according to what others would say to me—"life." My spark came back. This is when I remember my sisters telling me, "Vanessa's back—it's you again." Not because of the way my body had changed but because I began to come out of the shell I was in—back to life. I was meta-phorically taking off the mask of my eating disorder, freeing myself of its deceiving spell I was under for so long, introducing myself to life again. The people around me began to see the real me again. I did too. I began to *think clearly* since my brain was no longer starved. I could engage in a conversation. I didn't forget things all of the time, and I could concentrate. I was finally able to read more than a para-graph at a time again—something I loved doing. My mood stabilized, my depression lifted and my anxiety went away as a sense of calm-ness blanketed my sense of self. My body was no longer fighting so hard to protect itself as it was no longer operating in survival mode. I began to wake up every day with a sense of vivacity.

Healthy really is beautiful

Once I was physically healthy, I moved along much further in re-covery. I was able to focus all of my energy and attention on doing the work I needed to do in therapy. Now that I was healthy, I was actually able to *begin* doing the work I needed to do in therapy. If you are mal-nourished and sick (note: you can be malnourished at any weight) in no way can you make progress in recovery. You cannot even *begin* to do the emotional work that requires you to be healthy in order to do so.

As I previously wrote, I felt uncomfortable at a healthy weight. I felt like I was in a "foreign" body—similar to a teenager experiencing adolescence. You just feel off. I didn't like that my clothes fit differently, I didn't like having to buy new clothes (that's definitely changed), my body settled into where it needed to be—the body of a woman in her twenties. I didn't like it. Eating disorders do this. To remain ill, to remain small—is to remain a child—somehow isolated and "protected" from the uncertainty of the world. To be ill is to be afraid of growing up, of facing life.

An ex-boyfriend of mine said something to me when I reached my healthy weight. I was complaining to him about how uncomfortable I felt, when he turned to me, put his hands on my shoulders, and said, "Vanessa, you look beautiful. You look more beautiful than I've ever seen you. I'm a guy; I want to date a woman, not a little girl."

I had never felt so good about being where I was—looking and being healthy. I wrote down what he said to me (not that I would forget it!) and kept it as a reminder to me that *healthy is beautiful*. Remembering that health is beauty, that strength is beauty, that *skeletons* are not attractive was very helpful for me. I remember reading something one day that really stuck out to me—it was an article directed toward eating disorder sufferers. At one point it asked the readers, *"Do you want to look like a walking mental illness?"*

God no. I had to continue reminding myself those things until I believed them to be true. Until I saw them to be true (remember—recovery changes your perspective on everything). I can see clearly now that health is the most beautiful thing that exists.

Tips on developing a healthy body image:
- Avoid mirrors if you must! Cover them with inspiring words, photos, etc.
- Think of everything your body does for you
- Think of all the activities you can do when you are healthy
- Wear comfortable clothes
- Practice relaxation techniques—yoga
- Positive affirmations
- Cut out clothes tags
- Self-care
- Ask a friend what helps them feel better about themselves/ their body—guys and girls

Today, I love my body. I love the energy I have when I wake up in the morning, the color in my face, the strength to run, to jump, to laugh. I love feeling alive. I love being able to think and focus and learn. I feel great. I love the way that I look.

When you feel good, you look good.

12 | Living Life

"You can be the most beautiful person in the world and everybody sees light and rainbows when they look at you, but if you yourself don't know it, all of that doesn't even matter. Every second that you spend on doubting your worth, every moment that you use to criticize yourself, is a second of your life wasted, is a moment of your life thrown away. It's not like you have forever, so don't waste any of your seconds; don't throw even one of your moments away."
—C. JoyBell C.

Living life without your eating disorder

"A life free of calorie counting. A life free of obsession. A life free of weight obsession. Of insignificant numbers. No longer defining myself, my worth, my happiness, my success—by a terrible number. A life free of anorexia. Free of bulimia. A life free of physical and mental torment and deterioration. A life. Does it still exist for me?"
—Journal Entry, 2007

I never thought I would reach a place in my life where I could actually say that I am recovered from an eating disorder. I no longer have an eating disorder. I am not sick anymore. I would imagine life without an eating disorder, or try to remember how happy I was before I got sick, but those glimpses of bliss quickly faded away as my mind was once again flooded with thoughts of obsession and disease.

Letting go of my eating disorder for good meant that I had to:

- Follow my recovery plan 100 percent.
- Be honest with my treatment team and many times trusting them in deciding what was in my best interest (whether or not I agreed with them).
- This goes hand in hand with "doing what I needed to do."
- Keep on choosing recovery. Again. And again. And again. No matter how many times I relapsed. Choosing recovery despite how I felt.
- Surround myself with support and connect with others walking the road of recovery. I cannot emphasize enough how crucial support is in recovery.

Letting go/coping with life without ED

As I let go of my eating disorder, I felt overwhelmed. I no longer had my "safety blanket" (or perceived shield of safety) to hide behind—to protect me from anything uncomfortable. Without my eating disorder, I felt vulnerable, scared, unsure—exposed to the world. I had so many feelings and emotions. I had to learn how to confront uncomfortable emotions and situations, how to cope with life in a healthy way. I could not keep avoiding life—it would only keep me trapped in my illness.

I remember asking people over and over again, "How do I do it?" "How do I cope with life without my eating disorder?" "How can I deal with life without holding on to my eating disorder, or at least a part of it?"

One of the most challenging things for me was to let go of *everything* that had to do with my eating disorder. As I discussed earlier in this book, accepting recovery means letting go of every aspect of your eating disorder. There is no room for an eating disorder in a life worth living. For a long time I would not want to let go of the last little bits of my eating disorder. I felt that if I just maintained a certain weight, or "held on to my ED *a little*," I would be safe. I would feel better. I would have something to hold on to, to feel secure with as I faced the uncertainty of life.

That never worked.

You cannot live your life with one foot in an eating disorder. In order to recover, I had to let go of every part of my eating disorder. Holding on to my eating disorder—no matter how "minimal" I felt that I was holding on to it—*always* led me to relapse. After relapsing over and over again and finally realizing that what I was doing would continue to give me the same outcome and I had to change what I was doing—it was only then that I decided to *let go of my eating disorder completely.*

I accepted that what I was doing wasn't making me happy—it was making me miserable and I only got more and more frustrated with myself—and I realized that I had nothing to lose. I knew what life with an eating disorder was all about. I didn't know what being recovered felt like.

So with that, I let go of everything that encompassed my eating disorder. I followed my recovery plan 100 percent. If I had a slip, or two, or several, I would do the next best thing and keep choosing recovery. One day after the next. With time, I began to experience longer lapses of stability and shorter lapses of "slips." I didn't exercise when I couldn't. And when I did, I stuck to the limitations/restrictions set up by my team. When my meal plan had to be increased—I ate what I needed to eat. I attended all of my therapy sessions; all of my appointments with my nutritionist. I followed up with my medical doctor, took my medications. I went to group therapy, even when I felt like I was "fine" and "didn't need it" (* this is a common trap!). Do not discontinue therapy or going to your appointments/support groups if you feel good. That is the whole point! To continue therapy when you feel well is when you can make tremendous leaps of progress—you are in the best frame of mind to address the issues at hand.

Therapy is not to be used only when you are in desperate need of help or find yourself in a crisis.

As it turned out, life wasn't all that scary to deal with. It wasn't hell. It wasn't "impossible" or horrible. It was actually amazing. Life *is* uncertain. And it is beautiful in its uncertainty, constantly changing, constantly evolving. Eventually, I learned to flow freely with life. Eventually, I learned to flow freely with life.

"As your faith is strengthened you will find that there is no longer the need to have a sense of control, that things will flow as they will, and that you will flow with them, to your great delight and benefit."
—Emmanuel Teney

As you let go of your eating disorder, you will learn how to cope with life. They go together.

13 | Living a Life Worth Living

"Life is not living, but living in health."
— Unknown

When you are sick in your eating disorder you are *living to die,* you are not *living to live*. Being fully recovered from your eating disorder means that you are living to live. A quote I would often think about and look back on when I was having a hard time letting go of my eating disorder was the following: *"I will lie in my grave, dreaming of the things I could have done, of all I could have been."*

There really is never going to be a better time than *right now* to recover. Remember, you can choose recovery *at any given moment*. So why *not* do it now? If you do, and you have a setback, just do the next best thing for your recovery. And keep choosing recovery no matter how long it takes.

"No matter how many times you fail, you are leap years ahead of those who are not trying."

As long as you never give up, you can recover.

Living a life of lies, of mental, physical, and emotional torment, is not living. Letting your eating disorder take over you is not living. It is dying. My friend Jan said to me once, "It is better to die with an eating disorder on your medical record than to die *from* an eating disorder on your medical record."

Choose to *live a life worth living*. Do not live to die. Live to LIVE. Do so by choosing recovery. You *can* do this! *You are worth it.*

Setting yourself up for success

Sadie Carlson, therapist and Clinical Director of Tapestry Treatment Center in Brevard, North Carolina, would often mention the importance of "setting yourself up for success" prior to leaving residential treatment. I asked Jan Lockert what a life worth living looked like to her, and if she believed in full recovery. Here is what she had to say:

"YES! I believe full recovery is possible and very probable, if a person gets good treatment and follows the long-term recommendations of their treatment team! A 'life worth living' is different for everyone, but I would say that it involves living FREE from self-deprecating messages, expressing your emotions/feelings openly without apology, being honest and true to yourself and others, and relaxing in the fact that you don't have to be perfect or do things perfectly."

Ensuring a successful recovery

"Set yourself up for success." I've also heard this many times, and I really like it. What does "setting yourself up for success" mean to you and how do you go about it? What would be your advice for someone who is getting ready to leave residential treatment?

Jan: This seems to stem for the "positive psychology" realm, and I think it is important to decide what is NOT an option anymore, in terms of keeping your safeguards in place. A good relapse prevention plan can help with this. This again speaks to the importance of planning ahead, being structured in your daily life, and asking for help if needed. The transition from treatment on any level is very difficult, and should be done as slowly and as well planned out as possible.

Many factors should be considered, in terms of challenges that will be faced during the transition process and life in general.

How long should a person be in therapy?

Jan: As long as they need to be! This decision should be made by both parties and all members of the treatment team; and I think it's important to always leave the door open for sessions as needed, as life continues to present challenges, not just in terms of the eating disorder!

What should a relapse prevention plan include?

Jan: A relapse prevention plan should include a general overview of situations, people, personal factors that may lead to "triggers" for symptoms, or thoughts that may lead to symptoms. We try to have patients identify red, yellow, and green flags, as related to danger, warning, and safety during recovery, and what to watch out for. Then, coming up with a plan to deal with those things, or how to avoid them if needed, and overall, how to deal with daily life in the most sensitive manner to keep recovery a priority. It should also specify actions to be taken, and when, for increased treatment or interventions.

What is your advice for someone who thinks that they will never recover?

Jan: Wow . . . This is a tough one, but the feeling of hopelessness is never helpful. First, I think people need to know, need to be reminded OFTEN, that recovery is possible! And to NEVER GIVE UP! No matter how many times a person has sought treatment or has "relapsed," there is always hope. I think each treatment provides something, in terms of growth and/or awareness, and I think each person needs to be reminded of that, and be encouraged. I would tell someone that no matter how hard, it worth it, and to NEVER GIVE UP!

"I've always thought of eating disorder recovery as moving into a new house. In order for the recovery and healing to sustain itself and to have any shot at maintenance and even permanence, you have to build a house that will sustain this new chapter, this profound transition, this life-saving move. You start with the foundation—wood, brick, concrete—of treatment and a support network; you add on the walls and electricity of healthy outlets like therapeutic arts or intuitive eating and intuitive movement; you furnish each room with choices and decisions that allow you to feel safe and healthy and thrive; and when you're ready, when it all clicks, when you realize your life is worth living in this gorgeous house, you move in. And as you sit with utter patience, you decide to stay."
—Caroline Rothstein, writer and body empowerment advocate

Being YOU—Embracing Authenticity

Recovering authentic self/ED therapy work

We live in a society which places so much emphasis on weight and appearance. How do we break away from that pressure? Developing a healthy body image and self-esteem are vital in conquering eating disorders—what are the steps to getting there?

Jan: Being able to work on and "recover" in terms of self-acceptance and awareness requires being at a healthy body weight (different for each person), and then being patient that the core internal work is what "seals the deal," so to speak. Remember that it's a process, and that it's not perfect, as life is not perfect.

How do you help a patient who has just reached a healthy weight? (Reaching a healthy weight does not "erase" a person's negative thoughts/image of themselves right?)

Jan: Patience and doing core work on self-acceptance, awareness, and worth are important. I think it's helpful also to begin to help each person to identity what their healthy body is able to do for them, how they feel both physically and mentally/emotionally, and how much more positive this is for their life goals. Constant reminders of this being a "process" and of how much progress they have already made is always inspiring. Helping to give a person the ability and support to give themselves credit is also important.

What is your advice to family members who want to support someone in their recovery?

Jan: I always tell family members to ask their loved one what they need, and if they don't know what they need, simply remind them that they love and support them, even if they don't always understand. It's usually "safe" to ask how a person is feeling, about their day, tell them about your day, etc., and not focus on food or weight. EDUCATE themselves!!

In your experience as a professional and eating disorder survivor, what would you say is "key" to ensuring a successful recovery?

Jan: Don't be afraid to ask for help. Accept that you are human and that life is not perfect; hence, you are not perfect. Be obsessive about following your treatment recommendations, and don't stop meal planning too soon. Be gentle with yourself.

14

Self-Awareness

One of the amazing gifts that recovery has given me has been the opportunity to improve my self-awareness. Self-awareness is defined as "the ability to perceive aspects of our personality, behavior, emotions, motivations, and thought process." For me, self-awareness in recovery included observing my thoughts, recognizing them as either ED thoughts or my own, being aware of what triggered me, and being aware of emotions and feelings as they came up in the present moment. I continue to practice cultivating self-awareness every day.

Self-awareness can be a great tool to keep you protected against your eating disorder. mentioned earlier how much mindful eating helped my recovery and enjoying food again. Mindfulness in my everyday life is something I suggest as well (it goes hand in hand with self-awareness).

This ties into *mindfulness,* which is basically being aware of the present moment as it unfolds, without judgment. I mentioned earlier how much mindful eating helped my recovery and enjoying food again. Mindfulness in my everyday life is something I suggest as well (it goes hand in hand with self-awareness). Since I began my journey of recovery, I started practicing self-awareness. This took me to self-acceptance, which essentially means accepting yourself fully for the person you are.

"True self-acceptance therefore comes from an acceptance of the things you like about yourself, and the things you don't. As a result, self-acceptance is something that you do. It is an active process that involves a willingness to experience thoughts, feelings, and emotions without denial or evasion" ("How to Love and Accept Yourself").

Unlike self-judgment, "self-acceptance works differently. It doesn't paralyze you; instead, it frees you up. A self-accepting mind is aware of one's self and doesn't get lost in the mirror of social comparisons" (Somov, G. P., 2010).

I continue to practice self-awareness and self-acceptance in my life each day. I have learned to be kinder to myself, to treat myself with respect and dignity, and I have practiced learning to *love* myself. (Years of self-abuse in an eating disorder require lots and lots and lots of self-love.) I am going to live with myself for the rest of my life. I never want to waste another moment hurting myself. Self care is just that—care. Care towards oneself is essential, it is not selfish. Audre Lorde writes this truth beautifully, "Self-care is not about self-indulgence, it's about self-preservation. On self love, Oscar Wilde could not say it better, "To love oneself is the beginning of a lifelong romance."

Self-love is not selfish, it is essential.

"When you are loving yourself by taking responsibility for your own feelings and needs, then you are filled within with love and have love to share with others—without needing anything back from them. We are loving to others only when we give to them freely and don't need anything back, which occurs only when we are taking loving care of ourselves and filling ourselves up with love. Rather than it being selfish and pathetic to love yourself, it is deeply self-responsible."
—Margaret Paul, Ph.D., best-selling author and co-creator of Inner Bonding®

One example of where self-awareness has helped me was realizing an old destructive tendency of *overdoing things* or pushing myself past healthy standard—striving for unrealistically high standards. This formerly constituted specific eating disorder tendencies (i.e. over-exercising) and in other areas as well—taking on far more things than I could handle at once (i.e., wanting to hang out with *all* of my friends *and* study a full load of pre-medical coursework *and* take a full load of psychology courses *and* be a full-time college athlete *and*... the list always went on). This would happen to me time and time again. Like an eating disorder, this tendency or "addiction" provided an initial "high," and naturally; soon after, came the spiral; one that would drive me back into the arms of the illness and exhaustion in every sense—mentally, physically and emotionally.

After years of stability, I found myself repeating this former destructive tendency. *Never get overconfident. Know yourself and listen to yourself. I dismissed this in this moment.* I felt so healthy, energetic, confident, jumping with joy in all areas of my life, happily dating a guy and loving everything—that I decided that after doing well for several years, it would be "okay" to push the limit *just a tad*. I did well in school with a full-time load of classes while working, and wanted to graduate early. So I thought I would take a semester off of work and take—double the class load. 14 classes. *It's not a big deal I can handle it,* I remember thinking at the time.

I was in for a big surprise.

*Note: Pay attention to that "gut" feeling. I find that for me, most of the time it is correct . . . If I am quiet, breathe, and honestly ask myself if this is something that I *feel* **or know*** is good for me, or if it is something that I truly desire, that immediate answer that seems to come straight from my heart is often the right one.

In this case, I sensed that gut feeling, but pushed it aside.

*It is important to *know* your limits and be aware of your triggers. In this way, you can rely on this knowledge if you don't happen to feel that "gut" feeling . . . or push it aside as I did. (Always do what you need to do to stay healthy, despite what you feel.)

Before taking on this absurd load of classes, I discussed this with my advisor, family members and friends. *However, I wasn't completely honest even as I asked them for their advice. Instead of asking them* something like, "Do you think it would be a smart idea for me to take 14 classes this semester?" I said something along the lines of, "So, I am thinking of taking an extra class or two in the afternoon since I have a lot of free time. Do you think it would be a good idea?" I asked those questions and received the answers I *wanted* to hear. I could not blame anyone for "not telling me it was a bad idea." It was dishonest and sneaky on my part (even as I went to them for advice on the matter), similar to how I had been when my eating disorder was in the driver's seat of my life.

* Note the *dishonesty* on my part. Warning sign.

It scared me a little bit after looking back at the dishonesty, the sneakiness, and manipulation behind my approach, yet at the same time, after going through that semester, I realized there was *always* more inner work I could focus on (more to ask myself, investigate, etc.).

In the midst of my frustration in that moment, I lived through a *huge learning experience* and opportunity of insight into my habitual tendencies, into getting to know myself more, getting to know my own limitations and tendency of overdoing/perfection which is important for me to always be aware of.

Self-awareness can help *you* know yourself better. It can help you get a deeper and clearer look inside yourself, learn what helps you and what doesn't help you, what your triggers are, what your tendencies are, and where you have to be especially aware of.

Don't let your eating disorder fool you.

Always keep your antennas up. Pay attention to these things:

Are eating disorder thoughts coming up?
Are you worrying about food choices or thinking twice about them again?
Are you slightly engaging in behaviors?
Is your eating disorder whispering in your ear?

Are you focusing more on numbers, experiencing thoughts or urges?

If you answered "yes" to any of the above questions, make sure that at least someone on your treatment team is aware of this. If your eating disorder gets to a point where it is affecting your everyday life, know that you are at risk for relapse.

15

Thinking about Going Back to Your Eating Disorder?

Read this first.

Remember: *Everything* your eating disorder tells you is a lie. The "best" anorexics and bulimics are dead. You will never be thin enough, good enough, or successful enough for your eating disorder. You will die before you get there.

If you are struggling with eating disorder thoughts, urges or behaviors, reach out immediately and get help—do not wait. If something like this is going through your mind, *"Oh, if I just lose a few pounds/ get to x weight, I will be fine/happier/then I can eat normally again,"* remember that it's a lie. It is all a trap. Everything your eating disorder tells you is a lie; it always has been, and it always will be.

Once you get "there" (your ED's goal), you will just want to (or even if you don't want to it might be too hard to stop) lose more weight. And if you get there, it still won't be good enough for your eating disorder, so you will want to lose even more. If this continues, your physical health not only continues to decline but so does your emotional and mental health. This will make the eating disorder thoughts louder and louder and urges much stronger, which will make it harder to fight your way back out if you realize where this is taking you again. Should you continue down your eating disorders deadly path, you will likely find yourself lying in a hospital bed (with a high probability of unwanted medical consequences) or lying in a grave. If you're "lucky" enough to be lying in a hospital bed and have avoided permanent medical consequences, you still have a chance to fight back. Then begins the long, long process of climbing your way out of the pit the eating disorder has pulled you into, and starting the recovery process *all over again*. That long and grueling and painful process that it will be . . . if you go back.

Do you *really* want to go through all the pain, misery, agony, isolation, and imprisonment that your eating disorder has caused you before? Medical problems, isolation, emotional instability, agonizing and saturated with irrational and painful thoughts Destroying yourself physically as a mean of what feels like the temporary "only way out" of the pain you are in? Missing out on life, laughing, family friends, hobbies, passions, dreams, enjoying the pure gift of being *alive?* An eating disorder allows no room for life. It only deprives you of it. The end of the line of an eating disorder is only one—death.

Mean disease

Eating disorders operate by irrationality, plaguing sufferers with more and more irrational thoughts the sicker they become. The "desire" or addictive component and eating disorder feeds (no pun intended) of engaging in behaviors, of reverting to the illness despite risking one's life, shows just how dangerous they are. *Engaging in behaviors (i.e pursuing thinness and weight loss) no matter what the cost. Your eating disorder doesn't take your life into account, it never will.*

Don't let an eating disorder take your life. You are of infinite worth. Worthy for the fact that you exist and are a miracle to be on this earth, all of your qualities that add to who you are aside. I can say to you with conviction that when you experience recovery, when you make it to the other side, you will not imagine the strength and confidence and worth that you will be able to see in yourself. You are already have that, but an eating disorder will not allow you to see so. When things get especially tough, and you lose sight of your strength, keep reaching out. Reach out to those who believe and you and will remind you of your strength (remember there are resources available at any time). Keep being 100 percent honest with the people around you, so they can help you in the way you need. Above all, keep choosing recovery, one day, one meal, or one moment at a time.

16

Struggling and Don't Know Why?

If you are struggling with thoughts or behaviors and unsure why, it is important to pause and consider several things. What are you avoiding? What is going on in your life right now that could be stirring up these eating disorder thoughts? What uncomfortable feelings or situation are you not addressing?

Remember when you have an eating disorder thought it is something to notice—not act upon (a thought cannot hurt you, following it through with a behavior does). Your eating disorder cannot gain more control over you unless you choose to follow through with behaviors that further strengthen the thoughts and urges associated with it (fueling its fire). It is necessary to work through the uncomfortable feelings and emotions that underlie your eating disorder thoughts in order to recover. Do not engage.

Here is a pattern, broken down into simple terms of how a triggering event leads to an eating disorder behavior:

Stressor/triggering event → Uncomfortable emotions → ED thoughts → ED urges → ED behaviors

As soon as uncomfortable emotions, eating disorder thoughts, or eating disorder urges STOP. Do not engage.

Ask yourself:
What am I feeling right now?
What uncomfortable feelings am I avoiding?
What do I need right now?

Do not engage. Avoid engaging in ED urges at all costs. If you are having trouble doing this, turn to your emergency plan to stay safe from turning to behaviors. Later, when you are feeling less distressed, you can review these uncomfortable emotions in a healthy way. The most important thing is to avoid engaging. Do not hesitate to immediately reach for support in these moments. That is what support is for, that is what your emergency plan is for, that is what coping skills are for... Herein lies the crucial and vital component of eating disorder recovery. Overcoming these moments and making the decision to choose recovery over your eating disorder and getting help when you don't feel like you are able to do so.

Eating disorder thoughts and urges may still be present during or after you do this. Remember, your eating disorder *has* been your coping mechanism. And in the moment, it may seem like it's the "only thing that can take this (anxiety/sadness/fear/__) away." It's *normal* to feel uncomfortable as you develop new, healthy coping strategies. Be patient. There are tons and tons of healthy ways to cope, providing you the opportunity to try many different things which you find work best for you. Remember, as long as you *do not* engage in eating disorder behaviors, you are making a lot of progress. The ED thoughts, uncomfortable feelings, and emotions will eventually subside the more you practice coping *healthily* with stressors.

Eating when YOU need to eat

This goes hand in hand with following your recovery plan and protecting your recovery *at all costs*. I didn't begin to "adjust" my own eating schedule until much later in recovery. Throughout most of my recovery, I stuck strictly to the meal and snack times outlined on my meal plan. If I knew that it worked for me (as I had seen while

---

in residential treatment), I was determined to keep doing it outside of treatment. Once moving back home, I continued to follow my eating schedule. My family is from Mexico, culturally it is accustomed to eat at different times than in the U.S. This is true for any situation in life though—flexibility around eating. In early recovery however, I made a point to be as punctual as I could not only following my eating plan but eating on schedule.

I looked out for myself. I stuck with my own meal and snack times, and happily welcomed anyone who accompanied me, didn't mind sitting at lunch with a friend or family if I had already eaten. It didn't faze me. I protected my recovery and did what I needed to do, what I knew was working for me. Later in recovery, I began making adjustments, moving exchanges around to accommodate events my own life schedule (a gift of recovery, having that back), and so forth. At the end of the day, the important thing was for me to me eating what I needed to eat.

In early recovery, I chose to stick strictly to the exact hours outlined on my meal plan. By all means, be as precise and as strict as you need to be for as long as you need to. For me, doing this provided the structure I needed in a world of flexibility I began to step back into.

"When it comes to your life and your happiness, you've got to make yourself your first priority! You should never settle for anything less than the best for yourself."
—Ashli S., one of my sisters in recovery

Do WHATEVER IT TAKES.

Protect your recovery at all costs.

Protecting your recovery at all costs means doing **whatever it takes** to stay in recovery and keep choosing recovery. This can mean having set meal times throughout the day, as I mentioned that I did previously. This means packing snacks and meals ahead of time if you have a busy schedule ahead of you. This means eating what you need to eat, every day, no matter what situation you find yourself in. This means staying within your healthy weight range once you get there, and doing what you need to do immediately would that begin to change. This means going to all of your appointments. Medical, therapy, nutrition. You don't skip these just as you don't skip a meal.

This means taking care of yourself. This means using different coping skills to cope instead of engaging in your eating disorder. That is what coping skills are for and that is why I include a list of hundreds of different ones at the end of this book. This is what you plan ahead of time so when the moments get tough, you have access to this easily. When this feels impossible, this means turning to your ER plan. When this seems ---, this means reaching out to your support people. This is why you create support, this is why they are here. This is why support resources exist if you are not able to locate someone via phone or in person.

This means no excuses. At the end of the day, either you choose recovery or you choose your eating disorder. It is not an easy path, and at the same time it is possible. It ends up residing in you. In your decisions day by day, meal by meal, or moment by moment. And, if you struggle, this means picking yourself up by the bootstraps and making the next best choice for recovery.

Choosing recovery, choosing life, choosing YOU over an illness that wants to suck the life out of you again and again and again and again. This means making a commitment to yourself that you will never give up on recovery. Ever. This is how you recover from an eating disorder.

It makes no sense to "fix" an eating disorder behavior with another eating disorder behavior. If you are bingeing, you can choose to stop *right now*. And continue to follow your meal plan/recovery plan for the rest of the day (and so forth). If you are purging, you can choose to *stop* in this moment, engage in coping skills to keep yourself safe, reach out (whatever it takes), and make the next best decision for your recovery. If you are restricting, you can *choose* to make a meal for yourself and continue following your meal plan the rest of the day (and so forth).

Yes, you can do this. If you slip, remember that it's *okay*. The best thing is, you get many opportunities to keep doing so, to keep getting better at recovery.

Don't give up.
Reach out and ask for support from your team, family, friends, or fellow friends in recovery. You are not alone!

Questions you may want to ask yourself if you are struggling and not wanting to let go of your eating disorder:

- If you want to continue starving/restricting calories now, if you want to engage in ED tonight, then WHEN exactly do you plan on stopping?
- When do you plan on gaining the weight you need?
- When do you plan to do recovery "all the way"?

You know as well as I do, that if you "put off recovery," it's just that more unlikely that you'll do it. Because you will continue to get sicker and sicker. You will become more and more depressed, weak, unable to do or care for yourself . . . until you are lying in a hospital or a morgue.

Recovery from an eating disorder gives you a lot of opportunities. The blessing of this illness is that you *can* choose to make healthy recovery choices that can lead you to living a wonderful, productive, and happy life, *free* of your illness.

However, once you reach a point where there are severe health consequences, even if you *do* want to recover completely, you might not have the chance to anymore. Organ failure, heart attacks, and esophagus rupture are only some of the very real and dire consequences of eating disorders.

I was lucky.
Many are not.

Do not wait to choose recovery. Your life depends on it.

Don't let your weight drop below your healthy weight range, i.e., "in the danger zone."

It is so important to maintain your weight within its healthy range (established by your team of health professionals—not something your ED decides on).

Remember, if you want to recover completely, you will need to maintain a healthy body weight. Dropping below your ideal range is dangerous. Not only does weight loss open the door for eating disorder thoughts to come back full-force, it indicates the beginning (or middle) of a relapse, unstabalizes you physically, mentally, and emotionally, and easily drags you back into a downward spiral.

Please keep this in mind. Do not cheat your meal plan. If you do so, you are only hurting yourself.

Work with your dietician and/or team about any concerns or doubts you may have. *Do not,* by any means, dip your toe into the unhealthy and dangerous waters of eating disorder territory. Dropping below your weight range is stepping into ED territory, which, like quicksand, can grab you and pull you downward the more you struggle against it.

If you give your eating disorder control, there comes a point where it gets out of your control. Do not take that risk. Protect your recovery.

Why risk it? Why risk your life when you know what your eating disorder will ultimately lead you to?

Priority: Recovery above all else

When I was in treatment for my eating disorder, I had to make a lot of decisions that kept recovery as my first priority. Dropping out of school semesters, transferring schools, and moving back home, where some of the very difficult decisions that I made, in that in the moment, felt like extreme losses to me. But I know that they were the best and only decisions I could have made to recover.

You have to choose recovery above all else. School and work, as important as they are, are ultimately things that can be put off. Your life cannot wait.

Fear of change

Changes, stressors—whether they be change in residency, change in your work schedule, a breakup, a new relationship—add stress to our lives. It is normal to feel anxious during times of change, and it is NOT uncommon to experience eating disorder thoughts or stronger urges during these times.

If you struggle during moments of stress or change, don't be hard on yourself. Forgive yourself and remember that your eating disorder is trying to lure you in when you are stressed out and in need of some sort of "safety blanket" or sense of security within the uncertainty of things. Realize that going to your eating disorder will *never* give you stability, and it will *never* take you anywhere but toward your grave. *ED is never the answer.* Do your best, instead, to find structure during change. Follow your meal plan, plan a night every week to meet with a friend to talk, get together with friends or plan an activity where you can feel safe and supported. When I was recovering and no longer followed my meal plan but had moved into mindful eating, I found it very helpful to go back to my meal plan and follow it strictly. It gave me a strong sense of safety, structure, and security in my recovery. Also, I was at much lower risk of bingeing if I ate every few hours and gave my body what it needed. This was always an important motivator for me.

Don't let your eating disorder lure you back during moments of stress or uncertainty. Instead, make an extra effort to enlist support and establish structure if you can anticipate an upcoming change, or throughout it. If you are struggling, take some deep breaths, forgive yourself, and remember that *it is okay* if you have been struggling. It's understandable that you would have a difficult time; everything takes adjustment. Remember that *right now* is a new moment to choose recovery.

Do not stress about this week or this month. All you have to do is focus on doing the *next best thing* **right now.** Do your best to stay on your meal plan. Following a meal plan keeps you safe—and it helps avoid binges by not restricting. Take this one day, one meal at a time. I know it's hard, but you are incredibly wise and strong. Do your best to take care of yourself and practice a lot of self-care—you need to stay healthy despite what circumstances/stress you are under.

Keep reaching out. Remember, **you are not alone,** even though you may feel that way. (Call a friend, reach out to your therapist, attend a support group, join an online support group, Call a hotline.) *You never need to walk alone.*

Surviving the holidays—
Have a plan in place for the holidays

Holidays are usually difficult for people struggling with eating disorders. Changes in routine, family members coming and going, changes in structure, food all over the place. What would normally seem to be the jolliest time of the year can seem like the worst and most dreadful time of the year. But that's okay. That will change.

During the holidays, I reiterate the importance of having structure and enlisting extra support. It is important to ask yourself:

- What support do I have in place right now? What do I need from them to feel better about the holidays?
- What can I do to increase my support during the holidays?
- Can you talk with my therapist about this? Can I set up a plan with her for the holidays to help keep me safe in my recovery?
- Is there a family member or friend that I can reach out to during the holidays so that they are aware that this is going to be difficult for me and can help me in the moment, supporting me to help me get through?

My advice is: Do your best. Definitely have support, reach out, and if you can have someone by your side who can support you (a support buddy) during a holiday dinner party or event, this can really help. Do your best to enjoy the company of the people around you and try to think of what is really important in life. Enjoy the company and love of people you are around and that care about you, rather than worry about the food on your plate.

Try to stay in the moment . . . and be extra kind to yourself. Everyone deserves to have an enjoyable holiday.

Tip: *Never get overconfident!*

Even if you are feeling "great," have gone x days without bingeing, purging, restricting, etc., it does *not* mean you can just quit treatment altogether. That's why I mentioned earlier that even if you reach a point where you are doing and feeling great, *do not* quit treatment (therapy, nutrition, group sessions, etc.).

Not quite yet. *You will get there.* You can get the best work done in recovery when you are stable and feeling well. Keep up with your appointments. Keep medical appointments and weight management appointments in check. Go to your support groups.

Most important, keep being honest with your team and *with your-self.* When you are ready to "wean off" of treatment, your treatment team will guide you/help you to do so. Stopping treatment altogether is like quitting a medication cold turkey because you feel fine. *This can backfire; in fact, most of the time it does.* Be patient. You are getting there.

17

Relapse Prevention

> *"By **failing to prepare, you are preparing to fail.**"*
> —Benjamin Franklin

Relapse Prevention Plan

A proper relapse prevention plan should address the nutritional, psychological, medical, and interpersonal aspects of your treatment. I suggest that you discuss this with your treatment team to make up a prevention plan tailored specifically to your needs and recovery goals. Here is an outline I made of what I believe is essential to include in a relapse prevention plan.

Nutritional
- Meal plan
- Ideal weight <u>range</u> (*not a number*) defined
- Sessions with registered dietician (*specialized in eating disorders) set up
- Goals clearly defined
- Contact info available (with agreement regarding communication)

Psychological
- Sessions with a licensed therapist (preferably one who is specialized in eating disorders) arranged

- Goals clearly defined
- Contact info available (with agreement regarding communication)

Medical
- Medical issues/problems that need to be attended to
- Medications (currently taking, names, and dosages)
  - » Psychiatrist if necessary
- General MD sessions set up—have an MD
- Goals clearly defined
- Contact info available (with agreement regarding communication)

Family/peer support
- Support resources set in place (define who)
- "Sessions" set up (ex., local ED support group once a week, online support group, chat with online mentor twice a week, etc.)
- Goals clearly defined

Emergency contact information:
Tips:
- If you are in a treatment program, I highly recommend *contacting* your inpatient team with your outpatient team. Have them be in contact with your outpatient team **before** leaving treatment. Ideally they will be in contact during your stay if you already have an outpatient team set up or will assist you in setting this up. Make sure that you do, this is very important, especially when first stepping out of treatment.
- Once working with an outpatient team, **it is important for the treatment team to work together**. Once again, they usually will do so, but I encourage emphasizing this with each of the health professionals you work with, sharing contact information and *making sure everyone is on the same page*. Remember your recovery is *your responsibility*. Be proactive in your treatment.
- I recommend **printing** and having a copy at hand of your

Relapse Prevention Plan, as well as making sure each member of your treatment team has a copy with them.

Keep your "antennas up!" As always, be *honest* with your treatment providers, pay attention to your thoughts and feelings and communicate any behaviors or signs that you are struggling. **Do not wait.**

18

Safety Net

"Surround yourself with only people
who are going to lift you higher."
—Oprah Winfrey

You have the power to choose recovery and happiness over your eating disorder. The choice is always yours. No one can make this decision or recover for you. At the same time, this does not mean *you should or have to do this alone*. On the contrary, you deserve help in order to recover. You don't have to do this alone.

I continue to have a close group of people in my life today who I know I can always count on, and—although many don't *understand* the illness—they were always there for me. They offered me a shoulder to lean on, were a friend to trust that I could call in the middle of the night; someone who would listen or do their best to distract me and help put a smile on my face when I was struggling. These are the friends I cherish so deeply. Friends who stood by me, and continue to stand by me today. They know who they are.

Having people in my life who believe in me, who I trust, and who I know can support me if I struggle with anything is key.

"Everybody has a home team: It's the people you call when you get a flat tire or when something terrible happens. It's the people who, near or far, know everything that's wrong with you and love

you anyways. These are the ones who tell you their secrets, who get themselves a glass of water without asking when they're at your house. These are the people who cry when you cry. These are your people, your middle-of-the-night, no-matter-what people."
—Shauna Niequist, *Bittersweet: Thoughts on Change, Grace, and Learning the Hard Way*

You can always choose your support family. If it's not your family, find others who will support you. We can't choose our family, but we CAN choose our support family. I'll always be here for you if you want to write to me.

Professionals take on the importance of a support network.

You can never have too much support.

Dealing with ignorance/People not understanding EDs or the recovery process

Parents/friends not understanding the recovery process: Advice for friends and family
Jan: Assumptions are never helpful. Educate yourself on the facts, and I would consult with the NEDA Web site, or some other credible source, for factual information. It's also very important that family members and main support people be a part of the treatment process, as much as is clinically appropriate. This helps to alleviate guilt and also opens the door to more honest emotional communication and expression.

Watch out for ignorant/uneducated professionals—Choose your support team wisely.
Jan: Not enough can be said for the importance of experienced and

specialized treatment. If a professional treats people who have eating disorders, but they don't specialize in it and have not had specialized training, I would look elsewhere. It's critical that a therapist make weighing their patient, at every session, a first priority. This is a strong determining factor and indicator of any disordered eating or unreported symptoms. A therapist should also always collaborate with a patient's medical doctor and demand that a full medical workup be done initially, with ongoing checks.

Build your support family

Keep reaching out to people who understand what you're going through (the importance of having a solid support network).

"Feeling" burdened is not the same as "being" a burden. They are quiet different. You deserve to live and to have those who care about you know what is going on and help share the pain of your burdens.

19 | Closing Thoughts

In order to fully recover from my eating disorder I needed to:

1. Be 100 percent honest with myself AND with my treatment team at all times.
   No lies. No hiding anything.
   Remember—every little detail counts.

2. Follow my recovery plan 100 percent.
   This was hard.
   Sometimes—a lot of times—I didn't want to follow recovery. I didn't even know if I could or wanted to. Sometimes, I didn't agree with this or that. I didn't like all the food I was required to eat, I didn't agree with the goal weight my treatment team had set for me, I didn't enjoy not being "allowed" to exercise, or only be able to "exercise" x minutes at a time, with restricted/limited activities.

   I didn't like talking about my feelings. I hated crying all the time. I hated feeling like a broken, depressed, sad little girl. I hated being a patient. *An anorexic*. I didn't like being the sick girl, etc. At the same time, I feared being healthy, being a woman, becoming *me*. I didn't get along with my family for a long time. I hated them a lot. I hated them for not understanding, I hated them for catching my eating disorder lies, and I hated them for being so—close.

   The moment I decided that my meal plan *was not optional,* that what constituted my recovery plan was like a prescription clearly written out by a doctor—or a recipe for my favorite eggplant lasagna—every little ingredient had to be put into the mix. I couldn't *not do* something, do something halfway, or pick and choose in recovery what I did or did not want, like I used to pick at food.

No.

If I was going to recover, I had to follow my treatment plan, as outlined by my treatment team—whether I liked it or not—100 percent. The only person I would be hurting if I didn't follow through completely, the only person who would in the end lose—was me. Either you recover from an eating disorder or you remain ill. There is no such thing as being semi-recovered or "kind of have" a mental illness.

Never give up. *Make a promise to yourself that you will keep choosing recovery over and over again. No matter what.*

When you experience slips or relapses, go straight to your recovery plan.

And stay protected. Use your resources, surround yourself with support, and set up a strong relapse prevention plan with your team. Remember to continue following up with therapy, nutrition appointments, and medical appointments. Set yourself up for success.

Then, take the jump into life. Fill yourself with your passions, what you enjoy doing, things that fill you with joy. If you're not sure of those things yet, take the time you need to explore different things. *What do you like? What are you passionate about? What defines you and gives you a feeling of purpose?*

Then, walk boldly toward your goals.

Confidently.

One step at a time

20 | What Helped Me

- REALIZING that I was going to lose everything in my life to this illness, including my life, if I didn't change NOW. Taking recovery and life ONE day at a time. Not thinking about the future, just thinking about that day. That meal. That moment. Now. *What can I do **right now** to get me to where I want to be?*
- Having support . . . my family and friends to really support me. Knowing that it was okay to need help and need someone to cry to and go to. I had to be around people all day to not fall into bad behaviors. I felt ashamed in that moment and embarrassed, but I made the decision to do whatever I needed to do to NOT engage in ED. That is key.
- Urges . . . I had them, a lot of them. And ED thoughts and urges will linger for a while even after you stop engaging in destructive behaviors. So having a secure strategy/plan in place when that happens is key . Like I said, for me, it was to never be by myself. Little by little, I started to spend some time alone. And those lapses got longer, until I knew I was ready to be able to be okay alone. Being 100 percent HONEST with myself and my support team also was key. If you're not honest, you're only cheating yourself and your recovery. ED thrives in secrecy, which is why you need to be 100 percent honest.
- I had a lot of slips, bad days, and so forth. Some of my worst

moments happened the further I got along in recovery. But, getting back on my feet every time, never giving up, helped me get better. Doing the "next best thing" for my recovery after falling back into ED behaviors helps.

- And time. Everything takes time. Recovery DOES get easier. I don't know if recovery gets easier, or you get stronger. Seems like the latter causes the first. ☺ It gets a lot easier, and life gets a lot better. Have faith! I was in the worst place of my life 3 years ago.
- If you keep fighting, if you pick yourself up after every fall and never give up, you *will* make it. If you need support right now, please get it.
- I didn't have a therapist or nutritionist for a long time after I left residential treatment, so I found other resources. Family members, friends in recovery, online support. Anything can work. Find what works for you.

Eating Disorders KILL. Recovery just HURTS.

"I let it go. It's like swimming against the current. It exhausts you. After awhile, whoever you are, you just have to let go, and the river brings you home."
—Joanne Harris, Five Quarters of the Orange

21

Life Isn't Perfect

But it doesn't have to be.

On the morning of August 4, 2013, I felt like my whole world fell apart. The sudden death of my mother has probably been the most difficult thing I have lived through. Though despite the pain of losing her, I know and believe that life is still wonderful. Life is still worth living.

Despite the infinite range of emotions I felt all at once throughout the grieving process—shock, confusion, anger, anxiety, profound sadness, and so forth; *I had the choice* to cope healthily or revert to maladaptive (eating disorder) behaviors.

I did experience eating disorder thoughts during those moments. I even felt alarmed and scared after not having experienced these in so long, though it is not uncommon to for thoughts or urges to resurface even after years of recovery. For years, I had coped with my eating disorder when I was feeling so terrible, so it wasn't surprising that I had experienced urges to turn back to the illness at that point to avoid or numb all of what I was experiencing in those moments.

When I communicated this to a therapist I had previously worked with, he said to me, "I understand that you are very sad, but remember—there are *always* different ways to cope. Healthy ways." As bad as I felt, whether it was in that situation that I was currently living or in another situation in my life, I knew that I *always* had the option of coping healthily. There are always different ways to cope.

I think it's crucial to keep this in mind. Had I not lived through recovery and learned everything that I did as far as self-care, self-love, coping skills, and emotional management, I don't know if I could have coped with the passing of my mom healthily. Recovery prepared me in many ways to face the challenges of life. Life really *is* wonderful. It is amazing and worth enjoying every moment of it. My mother's loss taught me this as well. Life isn't perfect or linear, just like recovery. That wouldn't be real. There wouldn't be any fun or passion or *life* in life; it would be simply flat. The ups and downs in life, just like the ups and downs on a cardiac monitor, indicate that you are alive.

So while you recover, and after you do so, always remember that life *is* worth it. Life is wonderful. And since none of us have a day guaranteed, we might as well live the best life while we are here. While you are fighting your eating disorder, or any other obstacle, just remember, you *can* make it. You *will* make it as long as you never give up. Know that whatever storms you may face in your life, you will be ready for them. Just take things one brave step at a time.

"*And once the storm is over you won't remember how you made it through, how you managed to survive. You won't even be sure, in fact, whether the storm is really over. But one thing is certain. When you come out of the storm, you won't be the same person who walked in. That's what this storm's all about.*"
—Haruki Murakami

Resources!

Academy for Eating Disorders (AED)
AED is an international transdisciplinary professional organization that promotes excellence in research, treatment, and prevention of eating disorders. The AED provides education, training, and a forum for collaboration and professional dialogue.
www.aedweb.org

The Association of Professionals Treating Eating Disorders (APTED)
APTED is an affiliation of a broad range of professionals involved in treating people with eating disorders in the San Francisco Bay Area, including private practitioners-psychologists, licensed counselors (MFTs), social workers, physicians, psychiatrists, and nutritionists.
www.aptedsf.com

Binge Eating Disorder Association (BEDA)
BEDA provides the individuals who suffer from binge eating disorders the recognition and resources they deserve to begin a safe journey toward a healthy recovery. BEDA also serves as a resource for providers of all kinds to prevent, diagnose, and treat the disorder.
www.bedaonline.com

The Body Positive

The Body Positive's mission is to teach young people to creatively transform the conditions in their lives that shape their body image and relationship to food and movement. We use our compelling and straightforward educational materials to help people adopt a Health at Every Size lifestyle, allowing them to enjoy healthy eating and physical movement in their natural bodies.

www.thebodypositive.org

Eating Disorders Coalition for Research, Policy & Action (EDC)

EDC is a cooperative of professional and advocacy-based organizations that is committed to federal advocacy for people with eating disorders, their families, and professionals working with them. The Web site promotes membership in the Family & Friends Action Counsel, an eating disorder awareness advocacy and lobbying group.

www.eatingdisorderscoalition.org

Eating Disorder Hope

Eating Disorder Hope promotes ending eating disordered behavior, embracing life, and pursuing recovery through treatment referral, information, and resources. Our mission is to foster appreciation of one's uniqueness and value in the world, unrelated to appearance, achievement, or applause.

www.eatingdisorderhope.com

Eating Disorder Referral and Information Center

The Eating Disorder Referral and Information Center provides information and treatment resources for all forms of eating disorders. They have an easy-to-search database that is updated daily. They do not promote one form of treatment or one treatment center; instead, their goal is to provide you, the reader, with all the tools necessary to make a personal and informed decision. EDReferral.com provides referrals to eating disorder professionals, treatment facilities, and support groups, etc. In addition, they offer general information to inform the public about the treatment and prevention of eating

disorders. They have been in business since 1999 and are highly regarded in the eating disorder community.
www.edreferral.com

Eating Disorders Resource Center (EDRC)
Eating Disorders Resource Center (EDRC) is a nonprofit organization based in Los Gatos, California, that links resources, information, and support for eating disorders in Silicon Valley. The mission of EDRC is to increase awareness and understanding of eating disorders for the general public and for health professionals; to promote early diagnosis, effective treatment, and recovery; and to advocate for mental health parity legislation and effective insurance coverage. It offers an extensive online resource directory.
http://www.edrcsv.org/

Eating Disorders Resource Services (EDRS)
Eating Disorder Recovery Support, Inc., is a Marin and Sonoma County-based 501(c)3 nonprofit organization that is dedicated to promoting community awareness of eating disorders, professional education, collaboration, and providing treatment scholarships to California residents that need financial assistance for treatment. If you would like to apply for a treatment scholarship, please visit www.edrs.net or call (707) 778-7849.
www.edrs.net

FEAST
FEAST is an international organization of and for parents and caregivers to help loved ones recover from eating disorders by providing information and mutual support, promoting evidence-based treatment, and advocating for research and education to reduce the suffering associated with eating disorders.
www.feast-ed.org

Food Addicts
Food Addicts in Recovery Anonymous is a 12-step program of recovery for people who suffer from overeating, under-eating, bulimia, or

obsession with food or body size. There are no dues or fees and meetings are open to anyone who wants to stop eating addictively.
www.foodaddicts.org

Gurze
An excellent catalogue which publishes and distributes a wide variety of book titles dealing with eating disorders. Free catalogues are available online or by calling (800) 756-7533.
www.gurze.com

Inner Solutions
Inner Solutions is a counseling service dedicated to helping people heal from food, weight, and body issues. They base their philosophy on personal experiences of overcoming weight problems and help people look beyond their symptoms and into the real issues that have caused them to overeat in the first place.
www.innersolutions.net

Jenni Schaefer
Jenni Schaefer is a motivational speaker, writer, and singer. She has carried her message of self-acceptance and triumph over adversity to the campuses of Harvard and Yale, to corporate leaders and mental health professionals, and to audiences ranging from teens to seniors, earning an international reputation for her ability to bring just the right insights and approach to each.
www.jennischaefer.com

Kaiser Permanente
www.permanente.net/homepage/kaiser/pages/f17425.html

Lucile Packard Children's Hospital Eating Disorders Program
www.eatingdisorders.lpch.org

Lucile Packard's Pediatric Weight Control Program
www.lpch.org

Mentor CONNECT

MentorCONNECT is the first global online eating disorders mentoring community. In addition to offering one-on-one mentoring matches, the free membership includes access to a password-protected, moderated, PRO-recovery environment with live weekly e-support groups, periodic special events, a wide variety of online-themed support groups, recovery blogs, opportunities to personalize one's own profile page, educational/encouraging monthly teleconferences and more.

http://www.mentorconnect-ed.org

The National Alliance on Mental Illnesses

www.nami.org

The National Association of Anorexia Nervosa and Associated Disorders (ANAD)

ANAD distributes listings of therapies, hospitals, and informative materials, and sponsors support groups, conferences, advocacy campaigns, research, and a crisis hotline. Contact: Laura Disicipio, executive director, at (630) 577-1330 or Anadhelp@anad.org.

www.ANAD.org

The National Association for Males with Eating Disorders

http://www.namedinc.org

National Eating Disorders Association (NEDA)

NEDA describes itself as the largest nonprofit organization in the United States working to eliminate ED. Its Web site provides information and links about treatment referrals and support groups, research grants, and educational materials, as well as volunteering, interning, and advocacy opportunities.

www.nationaleatingdisorders.org

National Eating Disorders Information Centre—Resource Library

A Canadian, nonprofit organization, established in 1985, which provides information and resources on eating disorders and weight

preoccupation. Includes a list of resources in the U.S., Canada, and international.
http://www.nedic.ca

National Institute of Mental Health (NIMH): Eating Disorders: Facts about Eating Disorders and the Search for Solutions
This detailed organization describes symptoms, causes, and treatments, with information on getting help and coping with eating disorders.
http://nimh.nih.gov/health/topics/eating-disorders/index.shtml

Project HEAL
(Help to: accept, eat, and live) A nonprofit organization that raises money for people suffering from an eating disorder who want to recover but are not able to afford treatment.
www.theprojectheal.org

Santa Cruz Adult Mental Health Services Program
www.santacruzhealth.org

Something Fishy: Website on Eating Disorders
This support site includes a chat room and listing of online support groups. It also features a monthly schedule of chat events, an interactive bulletin board, and a treatment finder that can be browsed by state and country.
www.something-fishy.org

Summit Eating Disorders Outreach Program (SEDOP)
SEDOP, based in Sacramento, focuses on eating disorders awareness, education, and prevention.
www.sedop.org

Healthy Coping Skills

Here is a great list of over 100 coping skills you can practice instead of turning to your eating disorder. (source unknown)

I added a few myself! Find what works for you.

- Listen to your favorite music.
- Sing a song.
- Write a letter to a friend.
- Read a good book.
- Visit or call a close friend.
- Reach out for online support.
- Look up positive quotes and affirmations.
- Paint or draw. Don't judge yourself. Trust the process.
- Play with clay.
- Sit with a map of the world. Close your eyes and point to a place. Imagine yourself there.
- Fantasize about meeting your favorite movie star.
- Give and receive a massage from someone you trust.
- Put on your favorite lotion.
- Take a bath with a book.

- Massage your feet.
- Call a friend and ask him or her to come over for tea and fun.
- Call a long-distance friend to say hello and catch up.
- Doodle, write, paint. Just create!
- Meditate.
- Put music on and dance around your room in your pajamas.
- Take yourself to a movie.
- Drink chamomile tea.
- Burn incense.
- Take a walk in nature with a dog. Borrow one if you have to!
- Organize your room. Clean out junk and redecorate.
- Take some clothes to Goodwill.
- Exfoliate your feet.
- Go out on the porch and write in the dark.
- Curl up in bed with a good book.
- Go outside at night and star-gaze.
- Take pictures.
- Write a certificate of completion for something that you did and post it on your refrigerator.
- Go for a bike ride.
- Go swimming.
- Take a nap.
- Ask yourself how you are feeling.
- Make a list of positive affirmations about yourself, or read one you've already made.
- Do yoga.
- Kiss and hug your pet.
- Kiss and hug yourself.
- Chant.
- Enjoy a hot shower.
- Browse in a local bookstore.
- Talk to a close friend about how you feel.
- Learn to do sign language.
- Paint your toenails.
- Go people watching.
- Take yourself to an art museum.

- Tell someone you love them. It's okay if it's your cat.
- Read your favorite children's book out loud.
- Hug someone you wouldn't normally hug.
- Say "I love you" in the mirror.
- Practice Tai Chi.
- Lie on the couch naked.
- Go to the library and take out a book. Get a library card if you haven't already.
- Hug a pillow.
- Lie with your feet up on the wall for 5 minutes.
- Stretch.
- Ask for a hug.
- Color in a coloring book.
- Volunteer for a cause you believe in.
- Make a list of everything you are grateful for.
- Lie around and do nothing. If guilt arises, let it pass.
- Buy yourself a pretty flower.
- Remember one thing you like about yourself. Say it out loud.
- Walk barefoot in the grass.
- Give your cat a neck massage.
- Practice juggling.
- Recycle.
- Wear socks that don't match.
- Swing on a swing set.
- Hike a mountain.
- Sit by the river. Dip your toes in if you like.
- Play in a sprinkler or in the rain.
- Bird-watch.
- Go outside and draw what you see.
- Make a list of compliments you have received, or would like to receive.
- Pretend you are a rock star for a day. What would you do differently?
- Watch cartoons.
- Practice an instrument.
- Start learning a new language.

- Watch a foreign movie.
- Practice calligraphy.
- Climb a tree.
- Write yourself a love letter.
- Call a radio station and request a song for yourself.
- Give yourself a manicure.
- Make funny faces in the mirror.
- Write down your dreams.
- Practice a visualization.
- Write a letter to your childhood imaginary friend.
- Make a CD for a friend.
- Plant a tree or a flower.
- Visit a farm and spend some time with the animals.
- Say no to something that you don't want to do.
- Think of one thing that you keep telling yourself is too late to do, and then do it!
- Take five long luxurious deep breaths.
- Watch a motivational recovery video online—there are tons!
- Order a free recovery buddy online to remind yourself that you are not alone! http://recoverybuddies.blogspot.com
- Move energy. Push your arms against a wall with all your strength. (I find this helps release a lot of tension.)
- Wear a "recovery bracelet" and make a promise to stay on the recovery track no matter what. It'll remind you to keep fighting every day, especially when you are really struggling.
- Look up funny videos or watch a funny TV show/movie!
- Look up motivational quotes.
- Practice positive affirmations daily.
- Be gentle with yourself.
- Practice deep breathing.
- Use weighted blankets. A heavy blanket can help you feel grounded, secure, warm, and safe. Just pile on a bunch of blankets for weight and put on some soft music, take some deep breaths, and FEEL the difference!
- Guided imagery, peaceful music, soft nature sounds.
- Clean out your car or closet (it will distract your mind to do

another task and you will feel more in control of your life).

- Make plans to be around friends! (Anxiety and depression go hand in hand. Make the choice to get out and distract your mind from whatever is making you anxious. Go enjoy a movie or a cup of coffee.
- Light some candles or change the lighting. (Too much light can overstimulate your brain. Changing the lighting can help slow things down and help you relax. Even if you are just watching TV or working on the computer . . . some lit candles can help bring a cozy calm. Lavender or cranberry candles really work for me!)
- Spend time with someone who makes you laugh.
- Embrace the season. Decorate your room, dress up, go outside if you can.
- Do something for someone else. It can make you feel great.
- Purge . . . your feelings. Write, blog, draw, paint.
- Take photos.

* at some time in their life, including anorexia nervosa, bulimia nervosa, binge eating disorder, or an eating disorder not otherwise specified (EDNOS)

References

Binge Eating. (n.d.). Retrieved February 10, 2012, from http://www.nhs.uk/Conditions/Bingeeating/Pages/Introduction.aspx

Bulimia(BulimiaNervosa)Symptoms.(2013).RetrievedJuly15,2013,from http://psychcentral.com/disorders/bulimia-bulimia-nervosa-symptoms

Eating Disorder Statistics. (2013). Retrieved January 21, 2012, from http://www.anad.org/get-information/about-eating-disorders/eating-disorders-statistics

Eating Disorders Still Claiming Lives. (2010, January 11). Retrieved February 21, 2012, from http://www.examiner.com/article/eating-disorders-still-claiming-lives

Gallagher, D. (2012, January 15). Should I or Shouldn't I? Retrieved March 18, 2012, from http://www.thebeginwithinblog.com/2012/01/shouldn't-i

Garfinkel, P., & Kaplan, A. (n.d.). Starvation based perpetuating mechanisms in anorexia nervosa and bulimia. International Journal of Eating Disorders Int. J. Eat. Disord., 651-665.

Get the Facts on Eating Disorders. (n.d.). Retrieved February 12, 2012, from http://www.nationaleatingdisorders.org/get-facts-eating-disorders

Going to extremes: Eating disorders. (2012). Retrieved February 3, 2012, from http://www.cnn.com/interactive/2012/03/health/infographic.eating.disorders/index.html

How to Love and Accept Yourself (Self Acceptance). (n.d.). Retrieved April 21, 2013, from http://www.eruptingmind.com/how-to-love-and-accept-yourself-self-acceptance/

Paul, M. (2013, February 26). Is Loving Yourself Selfish or Self-Responsible? Retrieved July 21, 2012, from http://www.huffingtonpost.com/margaret-paul-phd/selflessness_b_2750730.html

Possible examples of Stockholm Syndrome. (n.d.). Retrieved March 21, 2012, from http://medical-dictionary.thefreedictionary.com/Possible examples of Stockholm Syndrome
Schaefer J. 2013. Life Without Ed. New York, NY: McGraw-Hill.

Self Awareness. (n.d.). Retrieved May 12, 2013, from http://www.pathwaytohappiness.com/self-awareness.htm

Somov, G. P. 2010. Present Perfect: A Mindfulness Approach to Letting Go of Perfectionism and the Need for Control. New Harbinger Publications.

South Carolina Department of Mental Health. (2006). Retrieved January 29, 2012, from http://www.state.sc.us/dmh/anorexia/statistics.htm

Wade, K., & Hudson. (2011). Get The Facts On Eating Disorders. Retrieved January 15, 2012, from http://www.nationaleatingdisorders.org/get-facts-eating-disorders

---

Contact Me!

I would love to hear from you!

Official Website:
www.vanessaschon.net

E-mail:
vschon.m@gmail.com

Recovery One Day at a Time:
www.facebook.com/WalkWithVanessa

An online community support page offering quotes, support, links to resources, articles and inspiration to motivate you throughout your recovery. The page includes a link to a private support group; a carefully monitored group to ensure the safety of each participant. The group requires permission upon acceptance; which either one of my moderators or I personally approve. Anyone can join, as long as they agree to follow a few simple general group guidelines.

www.ingramcontent.com/pod-product-compliance
Lightning Source LLC
Chambersburg PA
CBHW070013300526
45794CB00001B/301